Manna

*The only food
that will satisfy those
hungry for God!*

AndyBooks Publications
P.O. Box 44264
Charlotte, North Carolina 28215 U.S.A.
www.andybooks.com

Copyright© 2003

ISBN 0-9743493-0-5

"Manna"

Available In:
Regular Print Edition
Large Print Edition
Audio Book - Cassette Tapes
Audio Book - CDs

Cover photograph by:
Kristin A. Coke

Cover designed by:
Megan C. Brooks & Kristina M. Lindemann

AndyBooks is the official bookstore of The Karl Coke Evangelistic Association and The Timothy Program International.

It is the intent of AndyBooks to provide biblical studies and resources for people of all ages to understand Jesus the Messiah through authentic biblical culture.

For more information and full listing of AndyBooks products please visit **www.andybooks.com** or write to: AndyBooks, P.O. Box 44264, Charlotte, NC 28215 U.S.A.

"Manna" is one in a series of books called

"Food for the Spiritual Man"

These books are written for Timothy students
in several languages of the earth. Their clarity is
uniquely achieved with explanations from
the original Hebrew language of the Bible.

It is the intent of the author, Karl D. Coke,
and his publisher, AndyBooks Publications,
that you would come to know our Messiah, Jesus.

Dr. Coke boldly proclaims,
**"The LORD is upright; he is my Rock,
and there is no unrighteousness in him!"**
Psalm 92:15

Dedication

To Karen, who became my wife December 26, 1962, which has been the second largest portion of Manna given me by God. The largest being Jesus. Thank you Karen. I love you.

June 29, 2003 (your birthday)
Charlotte, North Carolina

Get Karen's music albums at:
www.AndyBooks.com

Thanksgiving

Special thanks must be given to:

My father, Butrus Abd-al Malik, a 1936 Ph. D. graduate of both Princeton University and Princeton Theological Seminary, for having taught me Hebrew and showing me the Grace of God.

My son, Douglas A. Wheeler, my greatest student, who, on May 25, 1984, graduated Summa Cum Laude from my alma mater, the California Graduate School of Theology, having written as his master thesis, "The Influence of the Hebrew Language, History and Culture on the New Covenant."

My brothers, Francis Clifford John Denton, a D. Phil. graduate of both Oxford and Cambridge Universities; John A. Looper, a D. Cs. graduate of Biblical Life Seminary; and, M. Lynn Reddick, a D. Min. graduate of Southeastern Theological Seminary and Ph. D. graduate of International Seminary–who, on August 30, 2002, on the rooftop (looking south at the Indian Ocean) of the teacher's apartments of our Timothy Program International–Rock Bible Centre Bible college campus in Muttom, Tamil Nadu, India, encouraged me to write this book.

My Timothy Students, who will read and improve this work.

My LORD Jesus, without whom I am nothing.

"Manna is a comprehensive Bible study of God's miraculous ability to supply man's needs. It clearly opens the meaning of *Manna* from Genesis to Revelation. It stimulates the need to better know God's Manna–Jesus."

Special Thanks

To everyone, since 1964, who has ever given an offering to support this ministry, **THANK YOU!** Thank you for sharing God's *Manna* with us. You have responded to God by giving us *Manna,* pressed down, shaken together and running over. You have now made this book possible. Without your help, we could not carry out God's call to help bring unity to Christ's Body and equip God's Saints for the work of their ministry. This book is offered as a small portion of our efforts toward those ends. May God's Presence be near you as you read. You share in the prophet's reward.

To Robert and Loretta Curtis of Lubbock, Texas, thank you for funding the release of the first editions (4) of "Hungry For God?" We pray that God will continue to bless all the work of your hands.

The LORD your God commands you this day to follow these decrees and laws, carefully observe them with all your heart and with all your soul. You have declared this day that the LORD is your God and that you will walk in his ways, that you will keep his decrees, commands, and laws, and that you will obey him. And the LORD has declared this day that you are his people, his treasured possession as he promised, and that you are to keep all his commands. He has declared that he will set you in praise, fame and honor high above all the nations he has made and that you will be a people holy to the LORD your God, as he promised. (Deut. 26:16-19)

Preface

Karl D. Coke, Ph. D.

"Manna" was written due to the inspiration of the Holy Spirit while I was preparing a sermon for the Restoration Foundation International "Feast of Tabernacles" service held at the New Temple Grove Ministries Church, Chesapeake, Virginia on Friday, September 27, 2002, Dr. John A. Looper, Director, presiding and Pastors John and Connie McDonald serving as hosts.

The sermon, entitled "Manna," blessed all in attendance. The conference keynote speaker, Dr. Mary Ann Brown, Dallas, Texas, also preached on the topic "The Holy of Holies." She prophesied about world impact. The Presence of God's Holy Spirit was so strong I could respond just one way. I committed to God, with His help, to write a comprehensive Bible study about "Manna."

The impetus to begin writing had come three weeks earlier while I was in Muttom, Tamil Nadu, India conducting a pastors' conference. The faculty included Dr. Clifford Denton, Dr. Lynn Reddick, Dr. John Looper, Rev. Paul Billy Arnold and Rev. J. G. Arnold. We were seeking the LORD every morning during this conference. The LORD spoke to us through Psalm 92:12-15. We had been listening to His Word to us through Dr. Lynn Reddick who said, "It is time for pruning." Interestingly, before sunrise that morning, August 29, 2002 I had heard God speak and had written down my response, "I will no longer attempt that which God cannot do." God cannot bless ministry He did not call into being. We were attempting to "prop-up" foreign outreaches which were depleting God's resources. We agreed to end those relationships and write.

So, with no guarantee of finances to release time for writing (away from public speaking–for which I am paid), or to pay for publishing a new book, I began months of research and contemplation on the subject, "Manna" as it is found in the Bible alone.

The process of listening to the Holy Spirit seemed to make me more a stenographer than a writer. I humbly offer you Manna. KDC

Foreword
Lechem min ha-Shamayim

Since 1964, Dr. Karl D. Coke's insightful teaching has challenged and informed individuals around the world. His mastery of the languages of Scripture, coupled with a profound anointing of the Holy Spirit, serves to produce electrifying interactions around the Word of God which leave hearers exclaiming, *"We've never heard it like this before!"*

Dr. Coke draws on his wealth of understanding Hebrew, the language of the *TaNaK* (the Hebrew Scriptures) and the thought processes of the Apostolic Scriptures. He also masterfully adds his considerable insight into the history and culture of the Jewish people.

Insights like those presented in *Manna* promote cohesion of understanding and relationship in the Body of Messiah. Truth liberates. Rightly-divided Holy Scripture is alive and powerful. When the Holy Spirit leads into truth, He prods the church to move closer to the unity of the faith. The words of life from heaven help the community of faith understand that "we are one bread."

Jewish people celebrate a rich tradition when they share fellowship and food while discussing *Torah*. As they prepare to eat, they speak the ancient blessing that Jesus Himself pronounced: *"Baruch attah, Adonai Elohenu, Melech ha-olam, ha-motzi lechem min ha-aretz"* ("Blessed are You, O LORD our God, King of the universe, Who brings forth bread from the earth"). When this blessing is said in unison by all present, it is believed that the *lechem min ha-aretz* becomes the *lechem min ha-shamayim* so that those who are in relationship around God's Word appear to be eating bread from the earth but are actually partaking of *Manna* from heaven.

As you read *Manna,* may your heart burn within you as did the hearts of those disciples at Emmaus who shared their bread with Jesus and in turn ate of the manna from heaven when He imparted to them a piece of Himself in the form of the prophetic Hebrew Scriptures. To eat of this bread is to live eternal life!

John D. Garr, **Ph. D., Shavuot, 2003**

Contents

"This is my Son, whom I love; with him I am well pleased. Listen to Him!"

——God (Matt. 17:5)

(Hebrew)

זֶה־בְּנִי יְדִידִי

רָצִיתִי בּוֹ אֵלָיו

תִּשְׁמָעוּן

Jesus

"He is the image of the invisible God, the firstborn over all creation. For by him all things were created: Things in heaven and on earth, visible and invisible, whether thrones or powers or rulers or authorities; all things were created by him and for him. He is before all things, and in him all things hold together. And he is the head of the body, the church; he is the beginning and the firstborn from among the dead, so that in everything he might have the supremacy. For God was pleased to have all his fullness dwell in him, and through him to reconcile to himself all things, whether things on earth or things in heaven, by making peace through his blood, shed on the cross."

——Paul (Col. 1:15-20)

Chapter 1
Jesus - יֵשׁוּעַ

Jesus is the "Aleph" and the "Tau," the "Beginning" and the "End." He is the "First" and the "Last."[1] Therefore, He is the first and the last chapters of this book. In the end, He alone is all that matters.

"He is the image of the invisible God, the firstborn over all creation. For by him all things were created: things in heaven and on earth, visible and invisible, whether thrones or powers or rulers or authorities; all things were created by him and for him. He is before all things, and in him all things hold together. And he is the head of the body, the church: he is the beginning and the firstborn from among the dead, so that in everything he might have the supremacy. For God was pleased to have all his fullness dwell in him, and through him to reconcile to himself all things, whether things on earth or things in heaven, by making peace through his blood, shed on the cross."[2]

Now, that seems to sum it all up!

The "church" spoken of above by Rav Shaul is both Jews and Gentiles who believe and confess that Jesus is God's "Anointed One" (Christ) sent to redeem mankind. "God was reconciling the world to himself in Christ."[3] This assembly of believers is made of Jews and Gentiles. Jesus was with Israel in the wilderness. "This is he, that was in the church in the wilderness."[4] He is and has been present with all believers. "For where two or three come together in my name, there am I with them."[5] "And God placed all things under his feet and appointed him to be head over everything for his church, which is his body, the fullness of him who fills everything in every way."[6]

In Christ, "there is neither Greek nor Jew."[7] "His purpose was to create in himself one new man out of the two, thus making peace, and in this one body to reconcile both of them to God through the cross, by which he put to death their hostility."[8]

Gentiles who believe that Jesus is God's Messiah owe a debt of gratitude to Jews who believe. The believing Jew has given the world the Bible, One God and the Messiah. As a Gentile believer, I thank everyone from Moses to Malachi for giving me the TaNaK (Old Covenant). This book containing the "good news" has clearly revealed God's Messiah to me. Now, "I am not ashamed of the gospel, because it is the power of God for the salvation of everyone who believes: first for the Jew, then for the Gentile. For in the gospel a righteousness from God is revealed, a righteousness that is by faith from first to last, just as it is written: 'The righteous will live His faith [Habakkuk 2:4].'"[9]

I am glad that God had both Jew and Gentile in His heart. He has always wanted them both to be saved. The LORD Himself says of His Messiah, "It is too small a thing for you to be my servant to restore the tribes of Jacob and bring back those of Israel I have kept. I will also make you a light for the Gentiles, that you may bring my salvation to the ends of the earth."[10] He also said to Judah about His Messiah, "The scepter will not depart from Judah, nor the ruler's staff from between his feet until he comes to whom it belongs and the obedience of the nations is his."[11]

I am one of those Gentiles who has become obedient to God's King Messiah–the one who hails from the Tribe of Judah! Like the Jew, Solomon (Psalm 91:2), I have confessed with my mouth that Jesus is LORD and believe in my heart that God raised Him from the dead. I have seen Jesus my Messiah just like Solomon (Psalm 91:16) and Simeon (Luke 2:30) saw Him before me. Like the Jew, Shimon (Peter) of Galilee, I have been saved by grace. "We (Jews) believe it is through the grace of our Lord Jesus that we are saved, just as they (Gentiles) are."[12] Like the Jew, Paul from Tarsus, I am justified by faith in God's sight. "For we (Jews) maintain that a man (Jew or Gentile) is justified by faith apart from observing the law."[13]

When Jesus asked me, "Who do you say that I, the Son of Man, am?" I said with Peter, "You are He, the Messiah, the natural born Son of the Living God." No one says that except God's Holy Spirit allows him to do so. He revealed Jesus to me and I confessed Him as LORD. Since that day in 1957, I have been hungry to know more about the One who saved me–God's Messiah, Jesus ben-Elohim.

Jesus is God's Living Word–God's complete Torah. "In the beginning was the Word, and the Word was with God, and the Word was God. He was with God in the beginning."[14] "He is before all things, and in him all things hold together."[15] "I was appointed from eternity, from the beginning, before the world began. ... Then I was the craftsman at his side. I was filled with delight day after day, rejoicing always in his presence, rejoicing in his whole world and delighting in mankind. ... For whoever finds me finds life and receives favor from the LORD."[16]

Since Jesus is God's Word, special care should be given to all the words spoken as Him. All should study God's Word precisely as Jesus instructed. Hunger for God's Word should be matched with a proper interpretation of God's Word.

Jesus preached the Gospel from the Old Covenant. His method of teaching and preaching reveals the proper way to study God's Word. "Beginning with Moses (Torah) and all the Prophets (Nevieem), he explained to them what was said in all the Scriptures (Ketuveem) concerning himself. ... Everything must be fulfilled that is written about me in the Law of Moses (Torah), the Prophets (Nevieem) and the Psalms (Ketuveem). Then he opened their minds so that they could understand the Scriptures."[17]

When one wants to understand a passage of Scripture he must first discover the foundational teaching about that subject in the Torah–Genesis, Exodus, Leviticus, Numbers and Deuteronomy. Secondly, this subject must then be found in the Prophets (Joshua to Malachi) to see how they apply the Torah. Thirdly, more information can be found about any Bible subject in the Writings–Psalms, Proverbs, Job, Song of Solomon, Ruth, Lamentations, Ecclesiastes, Esther, Daniel, Ezra/Nehemiah and I & II Chronicles. Scripture interprets Scripture. That is how Jesus studied and then taught.

Additionally, one will find more information about the above mentioned passage in the Gospels. Comparisons should be made between the synoptics, Matthew, Mark and Luke with John. Then more information can help clarify this passage from the Acts of the Apostles and their letters (Epistles) to the churches. Finally, more clarity on the subject can be gleaned from the Book of Revelation.

There are four additional insights in the New Covenant suggesting how to better study and understand God's Word.

1. Illustrations

The Jews in the Diaspora were told in Hebrews chapter 9 that the regulations for worship in the earthly tabernacle of Moses were *illustrations* for the present time. They were told, "The Holy Spirit was showing by this that the way into the Most Holy Place had not yet been disclosed ... indicating that the gifts and sacrifices being offered were not able to clear the conscience of the worshipper."[18]

The Hebrew words translated *"illustration"* in Hebrews 9:9 are *Zeh Hu* (זֶה הוּא) and literally mean "This (is) He." Therefore, Old Covenant passages explaining things like "worship" (for example) are the Holy Spirit's method of revealing what Messiah would be and do. Therefore, one should study the Old Covenant eagerly looking for the "This is He" passages and compare them to the New Covenant passages where Jesus is more fully revealed. To ensure this full revelation of Jesus, He promised His disciples that the Bible's Author, the Holy Spirit, would "teach you all things and will remind you of everything I have said to you."[19]

2. Examples

The believers in Corinth were told in I Corinthians chapter 10 that what happened to the Israelis "occurred as *examples* to keep us from setting our hearts on evil things."[20]

The Hebrew word translated *example* in I Corinthians 10:6 & 11 is the word *Moh-Pheyt* (מוֹפֵת) and means *"a sign of a future event. ... a sign, a proof,* as of divine protection, Psa. 71:7; ... and it is often used of the sign given by a prophet, to cause that which has been predicted or promised to be believed."[21]

One should study the Old Covenant looking for "signs" and "proofs" of what God does for those who obey or disobey Him. In the New Covenant we are asked not to disobey God as did those who are our *examples.* A great way to study Scriptures is to look for instructions which will prevent us from sinning against Him!

3. Testimony

One feast day, Jesus was in Jerusalem near the Sheep Gate pool called in Aramaic "Bethesda." On that Sabbath day, He healed a man who had been an invalid for thirty-eight years. This caused some Jews to question Jesus. In John 5:27 Jesus responded to them by claiming to be "The Son of Man," a Jewish Messianic title. This led these Jews to question Jesus about any *testimony* which would indicate who He was. Jesus told these Jews in John chapter 5 that the Scriptures testified of Him. Speaking of the Old Covenant, He said, "These are the Scriptures that *testify* about me."[22]

The Hebrew word translated *"testify"* in John 5:39 is the word *Moh-Ey-Deem* (מוֹעֲדִים) and specifically means "set times." It is used in John 5:39 in its plural form. This is the exact word used by God in Leviticus 23:2 where He speaks of His Feasts being His "set times" ("appointed feasts" in NIV). Studying the Scriptures looking for passages that clearly reveal the Messiah's appearing in ways and times set by God is thrilling. In this manner of study one discovers abundant *testimony* describing the appearances of Messiah.

4. Shadows

The believers in Colossae were told in Colossians chapter 2 that the Jewish regulations were a *shadow* of the reality of Messiah. No one is to be judged on how they keep these regulations because "they lack any value in restraining sensual indulgence."[23]

The Hebrew word translated *"shadow"* in Colossians 2:17 is the word *Tzeh-Lehm* (צֶלֶם) and comes from the root meaning of "being shady." "It is meta. used of anything vain, Psal. 73:20."[24] It is best used for the word "image" as is the case found in Genesis 1:26-27.

A good question to be asked when studying the Old Covenant is: **"Who is casting this shadow?"** The Old Covenant is filled with passages where the *"shadows"* of the Messiah are fully cast. These Messianic *"shadows"* are cast upon the Old Covenant from a pre-creation existence of the Messiah. God is Light. Jesus is the one causing the *"shadows."* The Old Covenant is the landscape upon which these *"shadows"* are cast. You will find His *"shadows"* there!

When the Bible is studied through "illustrations," "examples," "testimony" and "shadows," Jesus the Messiah is revealed. Since Jesus is the Word, it stands to reason that the Word should reveal Him. Therefore, studying the Bible should have the purpose of discovering undeniable testimony about Jesus (John 5:39). "For the **testimony** of Jesus is the spirit of prophecy."[25]

Also, "His divine power has given us everything we need for life and godliness through our knowledge of him who called us by his own glory and goodness. Through these he has given us his very great and precious promises, so that through them you may participate in the divine nature and escape the corruption in the world caused by evil desires."[26]

"This is what the LORD says—your Redeemer, the Holy One of Israel: 'I am the LORD your God, who teaches you what is best for you, who directs you in the way you should go. If only you had paid attention to my commands, your peace would have been like a river, your righteousness like the waves of the sea.'"[27]

"The Sovereign LORD has given me an instructed tongue, to know the word that sustains the weary. He wakens me morning by morning, wakens my ear to listen like one being taught."[28]

Studying Scripture by "illustrations," "examples," "testimony" and "shadows" forms a study grouping of **four** methods. This manner of study possibly answers why The Apostle Paul told a young minister, Timothy, the **four** benefits of Scriptural study. He said in II Timothy 3:14-17, "But as for you, continue in what you have learned and have become convinced of, because you know those from whom you have learned it, and how from infancy you have known the holy Scriptures, which are able to make you wise for salvation through faith in Christ Jesus. All Scripture is God-breathed and is useful for [1] teaching, [2] rebuking, [3] correcting and [4] training in righteousness, so that the man of God may be thoroughly equipped for every good work."

These four categories are clearly evident in the life of Abraham 400 years before Moses. God said, "Abraham obeyed me and kept my requirements, my commands, my decrees and my laws."[29]

One final study insight. "We have the word of the prophets made more certain" (II Peter 1:19). The context of this phrase is about God's Light shining down upon Jesus when He declared, "This is My Son." It is also a context for proper biblical interpretation.

Jesus Christ pre-existed creation. God, the Father, is Light. God as light shined upon Jesus at the dawn of creation. The Light cast a shadow of Jesus Christ across the landscape of the Old Covenant. Jesus, in the form of the Messiah's shadow, is found everywhere in the Torah, Prophets and the Writings.

When the Gospels were written, Jesus had been born, lived, ministered, died, resurrected and ascended. All of these physical events were real, not shadows. These real events made the word of the Old Covenant prophets more certain. He Who had caused the "shadows" is now revealed in full light. The Gospels are "high noon."

The Gospels reveal Jesus as the Messiah in full light. In the Gospels, the Light from the dawn of creation's horizon has now reached "high noon." The Gospels reveal Jesus as Messiah from directly overhead. The Light is shining directly down upon Jesus when His Father claims Him as His Son. When the sun is directly overhead, all objects lose their shadows. "High noon" sunshine casts no shadows. Jesus and His Messianic shadows in the Old Covenant become one and the same in the Gospels.

Peter said in II Peter 1:16-21, "We did not follow cleverly invented stories when we told you about the power and coming of our Lord Jesus Christ, but we were eyewitnesses of his majesty. For he received honor and glory from God the Father when the voice came to him from the Majestic Glory, saying, 'This is my Son, whom I love: with him I am well pleased.' We ourselves heard this voice that came from heaven when we were with him on the sacred mountain. And we have the word of the prophets made more certain, and you would do well to pay attention to it, as to a light shining in a dark place, until the day dawns and the morning star rises in your hearts. Above all, you must understand that no prophecy of Scripture came about by the prophet's interpretation. For prophecy never had its origin in the will of man, but men spoke from God as they were carried along by the Holy Spirit."

Before You Read On!

Take This Exam

1 In Whom does the fullness of God dwell?
2 What two groups of believers form God's church?
3 Where are the foundations of all biblical passages found?
4 What four methods can be used to discover Jesus in the Old Covenant?
5 What is the purpose of Bible study?

Read Before Reading Chapter 2

Exodus 16

Numbers 11

Deuteronomy 8

Do A Spiritual Exercise

Before you proceed on to Chapter 2, "Manna in the Torah," it would be helpful to log on a piece of paper how many times you "grumbled" over the LORD's provision in your life. By comparison, log how many times He has miracously provided for your needs. How has He done?

Manna
in the Torah

"In the evening you will know that it was the LORD who brought you out of Egypt, and in the morning you will see the glory of the LORD, because he has heard your grumbling against him."

——Moses & Aaron (Exo. 16:6-7)

Chapter 2
Manna in the Torah

We shall now begin our study of *Manna*. We shall follow the Bible's teaching on *Manna* in the Torah, Prophets, Writings, Gospels, Epistles and the Revelation.

Problem! Non-believers do not like miracles. In stark contrast with those who believe God's Word, non-believers have tried to explain that *Manna* comes from the natural world. The following article is a pathetic example.

"Some, drawing an analogy between the manna and the quails, which also miraculously descended to the children of Israel, contend that, like the latter, the manna was a phenomenon of nature which sometimes occurs in the wilderness of Sinai. Something similar is stated by Josephus (Ant. 3:26ff): 'And to this very day all that region is watered by a rain like to that which then the Deity sent down for men's sustenance.' As early as from the time of St. Anthony (c.250-355 c.e.), Christian pilgrims tell of a tradition, current among the monks of the monastery of St. Catherine in Sinai, that the biblical manna comes from the secretion of insects on the branches of tamarisk trees, which to this day grow in the wadis of the southern Sinai mountains."[30]

Why do men attempt natural explanations of such obvious miraculous events? There are many things wrong with the above explanation for *Manna*. First, it lacks the biblical features of *Manna*. Secondly, the nutritional value of the above explanation of insect cocci being *Manna* lacks the protein contained in bread. Thirdly, the volume described above couldn't feed one family let alone a nation! But, fourthly, and most grievous, by offering a natural explanation for the source of *Manna,* non-believers deny the existence of Jesus, who said, "I am He, the bread *(Manna)* who came down from heaven." It is also very offensive when the faithless author quotes Josephus and the St. Catherine monks for validation.

The foundational Torah teaching on *Manna* is found in Exodus 16, Numbers 11 and Deuteronomy 8. The following information will help expose *Manna's* foundations. Allow God's Holy Spirit to reveal Jesus as the Living *Manna* (a "Zeh Hu" ill.) from His Torah.

Description

In Exodus 16

v. 04 - Bread rained down from heaven to be gathered daily.
v. 07 - Glory of the LORD.
v. 14 - Thin flakes like frost following the morning dew.
v. 21 - Melted when the sun grew hot.
v. 23 - Could be baked or boiled (put in fire or water).
v. 31 - Bread, white like coriander seed.
v. 31 - Tasted like wafers made with honey.

In Numbers 11

v. 07 - Like coriander seed.
v. 07 - Looked like resin.
v. 08 - Could be ground in a handmill or crushed in a mortar.
v. 08 - Could be boiled in a pot or baked into cakes in an oven.
v. 08 - Tasted like something made with olive oil.

Purposes (beyond nutritional)

In Exodus 16:4

"To see if they [Israel] will follow God's instructions [Torah]."

In Deuteronomy 8:3

"To teach you [Israel] that man does not live by bread alone but on every word that comes from the mouth of the LORD."

In Deuteronomy 8:16

"To humble and to test you [Israel]
so that in the end it might go well with you."

God's purpose in giving *Manna* to Israel was not just its nutritional value. He wanted to "see" if they would follow His Torah, "teach" them that man does not live by bread alone and "test" them so that in the end it would go well with them.

Feeding Israel *Manna* was God's great equalizer. All Israel ate *Manna*. Moses and his family did not have their meals catered. They also ate *Manna*–daily. No man is exempted from God's "view," "lesson" or "testing."

Israel was placed in the wilderness where they could not provide for themselves. God led them into and in the wilderness.[31] The wilderness was another of God's great equalizers. "Wilderness" in Hebrew is מִדְבָּר (Mid-bar). It means, "(1) an uninhabited plain country, *fit for feeding flocks,* ... (2) *a sterile, sandy country,* ... (3) poetically the instrument of speech (from דָבַר to speak), *the mouth.*"[32] The word "wilderness" in Hebrew can mean "the place God speaks."

The way God spoke to Israel in the wilderness was *Manna.* In Exodus 16:15 the word translated *Manna* comes from the two Hebrew words מָן הוּא (Mahn Hu). "Mahn" is "from the root [mah-nan] מָנַן."[33] This unused Hebrew root word primarily means "divide or allot,"[34] "part or portion"[35] or most clearly "it is a portion."[36] "Hu" is the personal pronoun in Hebrew for the English word "he." Since God said in Exodus 16:4, "I will rain down bread from heaven," when the Israelis saw this bread, they called it Mahn Hu (*Manna*).[37] They literally called what they expected to see "a portion of Him."

Manna, a portion of God, was given to Israel to see if they would; 1) follow His Torah; 2) learn to live by every Word that came from His mouth; and so that; 3) it would go well with them in the end.

Manna was given to Israel for communication purposes. Why? Israel grumbled about God's ability to provide. *Manna* resulted from the grumbling of Israel. To "grumble" (Murmur KJV) in Hebrew is *"to show oneself obstinate, to be stubborn* (the signification of remaining and persisting applied in a bad sense); hence, *to murmur, to complain."*[38] Moses told the Israelis, "You are not grumbling against us, but against the LORD."[39] Therefore, The LORD gave them *Manna* to see if they would learn and follow His Voice.

The Torah "Speaks" of Messiah (Jesus) - John 5:39

We begin to see how the Torah "speaks" of Messiah with the phrase "Follow His Voice." Which manifestation of the One God is His voice? It is clear from Genesis 1 that God manifests Himself as God the Father ("In the beginning God"), God the Son ("And God said") and God the Spirit ("God's Spirit moved"). The Voice of God to be followed is the Son (Word) of God. God gave them *Manna* (Jesus - John 6) to see if they would follow Him (God's Voice).

Again, *Manna* was given to see if Israel would follow God's Instructions (Ex. 16:4). Why did God choose *Manna* to "see if the Israelis would follow His Torah (Instructions)?" It makes what God provides a life or death matter. The Israelis got that idea as revealed by their grumbling. "The whole community grumbled against Moses and Aaron. The Israelites said to them, 'If only we had died by the LORD's hand in Egypt! There we sat around pots of meat and ate all the food we wanted, but you have brought us out into this desert to starve this entire assembly to death.'"[40] Actually, they got it right! Yes, God does want us to die to ourselves in order to get all that we need from every Word that proceeds from His mouth! God is saying, "Will you follow My instructions and live?" Jesus is the Living Torah who, if accepted, brings eternal life!

Yet again, God said (Ex. 16:7) to the Israelis concerning *Manna,* "In the morning, you will see the 'Glory of the LORD.'" God called *Manna* the "Glory" of the LORD. Who is the "Glory" of the LORD?

John, the disciple whom Jesus loved, saw the New Jerusalem and said, "I did not see a temple in the city, because the Lord God Almighty and the Lamb are its temple. The city does not need the sun or the moon to shine on it, for the glory of God gives it light, and the Lamb is its light."[41] John saw the **"Glory" of God** and said it was the Lamb of God. According to John the Revelator, Jesus, the Lamb of God, is the "Glory" of the LORD!

David, the man after God's own heart, when praising God toward His holy temple, said, "May all the kings of the earth praise you, O LORD when they hear the words of your mouth. May they sing of the ways of the LORD, for the **glory of the LORD** is great."[42]

Habukkuk, the Jewish prophet who inspired the Apostle Paul and Martin Luther, said, "the righteous shall live by his faith," and "For the earth will be filled with the knowledge of the **glory of the LORD,** as the waters cover the sea."[43] Rabbi Telushkin says of the Book of Habukkuk, "Among the book's most enduring influential verses is Habukkuk's prophecy of a future day when 'the earth will be filled with the knowledge of the glory of the Lord, as the waters cover the sea' (2:14; see Isaiah 11:9). The Babylonian Talmud (*Makkot* 24a) cites the prophet's statement that the 'righteous shall live by his faith' (2:4) as a one-sentence summary of all the Torah's commandments."[44]

Ezekiel, the Jewish prophet who describes Israel and Jerusalem after the return of Messiah, saw Him, the Glory of the LORD. He said, while standing by the River Kebar, "Then there came a voice from above the expanse over their heads as they (angels) stood with lowered wings. Above the expanse over their heads was what looked like a throne of sapphire, and high above the throne was a figure like that of a man. I saw that from what appeared to be his waist up he looked like flowing metal, as if full of fire; and brilliant light surrounded him. Like the appearance of a rainbow in the clouds on a rainy day, so was the radiance around him. This was the appearance of the likeness of the **glory of the LORD.** When I saw it, I fell facedown, and I heard the voice of one speaking."[45]

Isaiah, whose name means "Jehovah saves," and who prophesied about John the Baptist, cousin of Jesus, said of John, He is "A voice of one calling: 'In the desert prepare the way for the LORD; make straight in the wilderness a highway for our God. Every valley shall be raised up, every mountain and hill made low; the rough ground shall become level, the rugged places a plain. And the **glory of the LORD** will be revealed, and all mankind together will see it. For the mouth of the LORD has spoken.'"[46] Isaiah prophesied that someone would be a voice in the wilderness calling for men to prepare the way for the Lord. John was that voice. John revealed Jesus as the **Glory of the LORD** when he said, "Behold, the Lamb of God, which taketh away the sin of the world."[47]

Notice again that the "Lamb" of God and the "Glory" of God are synonyms describing Jesus–God's heavenly bread–*Manna.*

The Israelis called what they saw on the ground *Man Hu*. This was due to what they expected to see when they arose in the morning. The day before *Manna* appeared for the first time, God told Moses (Ex. 16:4), "I will rain down bread from heaven for you." The Hebrew text reads: הִנְנִי מַמְטִיר לָכֶם מִן־הַשָּׁמָיִם (hin-nee mam-teer lechem min hash-sha-ma-yim). The literal translation of this passage is: "See, I will rain down–bread from heaven(s)." The LORD God put the expectation in the heart of Moses that He, God, would be raining down from heaven manifested as bread. The Israelis expected God to rain down from heaven. This explains why (v. 15) they called what they saw *"Man Hu"*–"a little portion of Him."

Manna has to be God manifested as Messiah Jesus. *Manna* revealed the Glory of the LORD. *Manna* was the Living Torah which was to be followed. Nothing makes this point more clearly than the process of gathering *Manna*. Moses said in Exodus 16:8 that when they gathered bread in the morning, "you will know it was the LORD." Note that each person gathered enough *Manna* each morning for that day's need. This should be the practice of every believer–meeting every morning with the LORD and then going about daily activities. God asked Moses for this type of meeting (Ex. 8:20; 9:13; 34:4). Jesus followed this practice (Mark 1:35).

Another revelation concerning gathering *Manna* has to do with *Manna* spoiling if one gathered too much on any day except the day before Sabbath (Ex. 16:20). That day, the Israelis could gather a "double-portion" of *Manna,* one for that day and one for the Sabbath. That excess would not spoil. The reason they had to gather a "double-portion" before the Sabbath was God said there would be no *Manna* on the ground Sabbath morning (v. 25). This "speaks" of Jesus, God's *Manna*, being buried on the Sabbath. This is the LORD's Day of Rest. God was not tired following His six days of creation. He rested on the seventh day to commemorate forever the day His Son would be buried in the earth. "The Sabbath was made for man, not man for the Sabbath. So the Son of Man is Lord even of the Sabbath."[48] Therefore, God weekly taught the Israelis for 40 years that His *Manna* would not be above ground on the Sabbath. Jesus, as God's *Manna*, did not spoil during the Sabbath He was in the grave. He, like the *Manna* Moses put in the pot for all generations to see, was alive, is alive, and so shall ever be!

This leads us to discover how *Manna* was to be prepared before it was eaten. It could either be boiled in a pot or baked in an oven.

Manna was useful for the Israeli's daily needs. It was useful when boiled. It was useful when baked. That is, it was useful when it passed through the water and when it passed through the fire. Therefore, *Manna* had to pass through (be baptized in) the water and the fire. We know Jesus passed through (was baptized in) the water by John (Matthew 3:13-17). We know from Jesus' own testimony (Luke 12:50) that He had to pass through the fire baptism of death, burial and resurrection. Jesus, having passed through the water and fire as God's *Manna,* is useful to all who take Him in.

But, before *Manna* could be boiled or baked it had to be "ground in a handmill" or "crushed in a mortar."[49]

Isaiah said of Jesus in Isaiah 53:4-5, "Surely he took up our infirmities and carried our sorrows, yet we considered him stricken by God, smitten by him, and afflicted. But he was pierced for our transgressions, he was crushed for our iniquities, the punishment that brought us peace [shalom - health] was upon him, and by his wounds we are healed." These words of Isaiah make it quite clear just how "useful" *Manna* (Jesus) is to those who take Him in.

Again, Isaiah said of Jesus in Isaiah 52:13-15, "See, my servant will prosper; he will be raised [resurrected] and lifted [ascended] up and highly exalted [seated at God's right hand]. Just as there were many who were appalled at him–his appearance was so disfigured beyond that of any man and his form marred beyond human likeness–so will he sprinkle many nations, and kings will shut their mouths because of him. For what they were not told, they will see, and what they have not heard, they will understand."

Praise God for Jesus the Messiah! Praise God for Jesus the *Manna* sent from heaven! Praise God that "it was the LORD's will to crush him and cause him to suffer, and though the LORD makes his life a guilt offering, he will see his offspring and prolong his days, and the will of the LORD will prosper in his hand."[50] Although God's *Manna* must be crushed and then pass through the water and the fire, He will accomplish the purpose for which He has been sent!

Before You Read On!

Take This Exam

1 What is it that non-believers do not like?
2 Why did God put Israel in the Wilderness?
3 What does *"Man Hu"* Mean?
4 Beside Moses, who also called *Manna* "The Glory of the LORD?"
5 Why didn't God provide *Manna* on the Sabbath?

Read Before Reading Chapter 3

Joshua 5:10-12

Isaiah 55

I Kings 17:7-24

Do A Spiritual Exercise

Before you proceed on to Chapter 3, "Manna in the Nevieem," it would be helpful to log on a piece of paper how many times the LORD provided items in your life that cost you nothing. It would be helpful to estimate how much money God has saved you on these occasions. How much?

Manna
in the Nevieem

"Don't be afraid. Go home and do
as you have said. But first make a
small cake of bread for me from what
you have and bring it to me, and
then make something for yourself
and your son. For this is what the
LORD, the God of Israel, says: 'This
jar of flour will not be used up and
the jug of oil will not run dry until
the day the LORD gives rain on the
land.'"

——Elijah (I Kings 17:13-14)

Chapter 3
Manna in the Nevieem

The second major section in the Hebrew Bible is the *Nevieem.*
"Nevieem" is Hebrew for "prophets." The *Nevieem* has two sub-
sections. The first section is called the "former" or "non-writing"
prophets. These four scrolls include Joshua, Judges, I/II Samuel
and I/II Kings. The second section is called the "latter" or "writing"
prophets. These four scrolls are Isaiah, Jeremiah, Ezekiel and Hosea.
The fourth scroll, Hosea, actually contains 12 small books includ-
ing Hosea, Joel, Amos, Obadiah, Jonah, Micah, Nahum, Habakkuk,
Zephaniah, Haggai, Zechariah and Malachi.

When the prophets preached Torah, they revealed God's purposes.
To do this, they had to be devoted students of Torah. God told the
prophet Joshua, "Do not let this Book of the Torah depart from
your mouth; meditate on it day and night, so that you may be care-
ful to do everything written in it. Then you will be prosperous and
successful."[51] Ezra and Nehemiah committed to this principle (Ezra
3:2; 7:10; Neh. 10:29). King David wrote poetry about this principle (Psa. 1). Paul taught Timothy this principle (II Tim. 2:15).

"Learning Torah is not a part-time occupation but rather a full-
time preoccupation, contiguous with life itself. Jewish learning,
especially for males, is considered to be an endless religious obli-
gation superseding all others. This notion is based on at least two
well-known proof texts, one scriptural, the other talmudic. In Joshua
(1:8) the message is simple: 'This Torah shall not depart out of thy
mouth; but thou shalt meditate upon it day and night.'"[52]

Prophets studied, obeyed and then taught Torah. Why were they
so intense in their study? "The prophets, who spoke of the grace
that was to come to you, searched intently and with the greatest
care, trying to find out the time and circumstances to which the
Spirit of Messiah in them was pointing when he predicted the suf-
ferings of Messiah and the glories that would follow."[53] Prophets
studied and obeyed Torah in order to teach about God's Messiah.

This book is about *Manna*. Jesus told us to study a matter first in the *Torah,* then in the *Nevieem* and then in the *Ketuveem.* Why? Because, "in the mouth of two or three witnesses a matter is established" (Deut. 17:6). In this chapter, we shall establish the matter of *Manna* with the witnesses Joshua, Isaiah and Elijah.

Witness Number One - Joshua - Qualifications:

"**JOSHUA** ... (יְהוֹשֻׁעַ, LXX Ἰησοῦς, *Yahweh is salvation*). ... The commander of the Israelites during the conquest of Canaan. **1. Family.** The son of Nun, he belonged to the tribe of Ephraim (Num. 13:8). He settled in Timnath-serah (Josh. 19:50; Timnath-heres, Judg. 2:9) in the hill country of Ephraim, and was buried there (Josh 24:30). ... Joshua served as personal minister to Moses when the latter was on Mount Sinai receiving the law (Exod. 24:13; 32:17). Joshua was in attendance whenever the LORD would speak to Moses in the tent of meeting outside the camp (33:11). From Moses he learned the value of the anointing of God's Spirit when he would have forbidden certain elders to prophesy (Nu. 11:27-29)."[54]

The Matter: "When did Manna end for Israel?"

The "ABC's" of the ending of Manna in Torah
Exodus 16:35
The Israelites ate manna forty years,
until they came to a land that was settled;
they ate manna until they reached the border of Canaan.

The matter defined by the prophet "eye-witness" Joshua
Joshua 5:10-12
On the evening of the fourteenth day of the month,
while camped at Gilgal on the plain of Jericho,
the Israelites celebrated Passover.

The day after the Passover, that very day,
they ate some of the produce of the land:
unleavened bread and roasted grain.

The manna stopped the day after they ate this food from the land;
there was no longer any manna for the Israelites,
but that year they ate of the produce of Canaan.

According to Moses, Israel ate *Manna* for forty years until they reached the border of Canaan. Joshua explains the matter more precisely in order to make God's intent for ending *Manna* known. What Joshua reveals about the ending of this provision clearly reveals Jesus as God's Messiah–the ultimate provision for man's needs.

Joshua's first point (v. 10) is that the Israelis (after entering Canaan and while camped at Gilgal near Jericho) celebrated Passover on *Nisan* 14. They were still being supplied *Manna.* The Israelis were still eating *Manna* on their first Passover in the Promised Land.

Joshua's second point (v. 11) is that the Israelis on *Nisan* 15, the day after Passover (called the "Feast of Unleavened Bread" in Leviticus 23:6), were still being supplied *Manna.* The Israelis were still eating *Manna* on their first Feast of Unleavened Bread in the Promised Land.

Joshua's third point (v. 12) is that the Israelis on Sunday, *Nisan* 16, the day following Unleavened Bread, ate the produce of Canaan. This is the day called "Feast of Firstfruits." This is the exact day God stopped supplying *Manna* to the Israelis. The Israelis stopped eating *Manna* in the Promised Land on their first Feast of Firstfruits.

Moses spoke about this matter generally by saying, "they ate manna until they reached the border of Canaan." The prophet and Messiah revealer spoke about it precisely. He said, "The manna stopped the day after [Feast of Unleavened Bread] they ate fruit from the land; there was no longer any manna for the Israelites, but that year they ate of the produce of Canaan" (v. 12).

Why did Joshua speak so precisely? To make Jesus, God's Messiah, clearly known. Jesus, God's Messiah, died on Passover, was buried during the Feast of Unleavened Bread, and resurrected Sunday, the Feast of Firstfruits. Jesus, as God's Messiah, provides everything needed for eternal life. This includes sinful man's need for Messiah's death, burial and resurrection. His death was for every believer. His burial was for every believer. Paul said in Romans 6:1-4 that Jesus died and believers died with Him; Jesus was buried and believers were buried with Him; Jesus arose so that believers could walk in newness of life–the life of Messiah Himself!

Witness Number Two - Isaiah

Qualifications:

"ISAIAH (יְשַׁעְיָה, *Yahweh is salvation*). The first of the major
prophets in the English Bible, the first of the latter prophets in the
Hebrew Bible, the largest and probably the most universally cher-
ished of the OT prophetical books. The prophet Isaiah is mentioned repeatedly in 2 Kings and three times in 2 Chronicles. His
name appears sixteen times in the book that bears his name. The
book is dated to the reign of Uzziah, Jotham, Ahaz and Hezekiah,
kings of Judah. Late tradition asserts that the prophet was martyred
in the reign of Mannasseh."[55]

The Matter: "What can Manna do?"

The "ABC's" of what Manna can do in the Torah

Deuteronomy 8:4

*Your clothes did not wear out
and your feet did not swell
during these forty years.*

Deuteronomy 29:5

*During the forty years that I led you through the desert,
your clothes did not wear out,
nor did the sandals on your feet.
You ate no bread and drank no wine or other fermented drink.*

The matter defined by the prophet Isaiah

Isaiah 55:10-11

*As the rain and the snow come down from heaven, and do not
return to it without watering the earth and making it bud and flour-
ish, so that it yields seed for the sower and bread for the eater,*

*so is my word that goes out from my mouth. It will not return to
me empty, but will accomplish what I desire and achieve the purpose for which I sent it.*

Isaiah compares *Manna* to rain and snow because they all come down from heaven to the earth. He also uses this metaphor to indicate where *Manna* works best. Rain and snow do their work beneath the surface. They act as the agent to deliver to plants what they need from the surrounding soil. When water is present, a seed will attract to itself everything it needs from the soil around it. It then grows into a balanced food product for some animal to eat and gain the nutrition it needs. Water helps a plant get all the minerals it needs directly from the soil. Minerals and water from the soil are taken up by the roots and delivered to all the cells of the plant. Snow supplies more nitrogen (fertilizer) to the soil than rain. Both are necessary so that the plant matures to provide nutrition.

Likewise, *Manna* works best beneath the surface–inside the heart of man. It is God's agent to deliver all that man needs. A man who hides the Word of God inside himself will be "like a tree planted by streams of water, which yields its fruit in season and whose leaf does not wither. Whatever he does prospers."[56] The metaphor of *Manna* being likened unto rain or snow is made complete when the fruit borne by a "well-manna'd" man is eaten by others.

How much can *Manna* do? What can *Manna* do? What form does *Manna* take? When God says, "'Peace, peace, to those far and near,' says the LORD. 'And I will heal them ...'"[57] can He give peace and heal? Can He really "supply all our need according to His riches in glory?"[58] Can we count on the fact that "he who supplies seed to the sower and bread for food will also supply and increase your store of seed and will enlarge the harvest of your righteousness, so that you will be made rich in every way, so that you can be generous on every occasion, and through us [Paul] your generosity will result in thanksgiving to God?"[59] Isaiah says "yes" to all of this. God's Word (*Manna*) will not return to Him empty, but will accomplish the purpose for which it has been sent.

The Name God gave Moses (Ex. 3:14) was "I Am that I Am." It means, "I Am whatever you need." It could also be translated, "I shall be there, for there I shall be." God's Word can be nothing less than God Himself. His Word can do "any" and "every" thing "any" and "every" time. God's *Manna* inside a man allows him to say, "I can do all things through Christ who strengthens me" (Phil. 4:13).

Witness Number Three - Elijah

Qualifications:

"**ELIJAH** (אֵלִיָּהוּ, *Yah is my God ...*) was the famous 9th century prophet who served in the northern kingdom in the reigns of Ahab and his son, Ahaziah. One of the outstanding heroes in the Bible, Elijah was prominent in Jewish prophetic expectations; representatives of religious officialdom were sent to question John the Baptist concerning his identity and asked him if he [were] Elijah (John 1:21, 25). His importance in God's plan for the ages is apparent from his predicted reappearing before "the great and terrible day of the LORD" (Mal. 4:5) and from his presence with Moses and the Lord upon the Mount of Transfiguration, where the three talked about the Lord's sacrificial death (Matt. 17:1-13; Mark 9:2-13; Luke 9:28-36)."[60] He is from Tishbe in Gilead (I Kings 17:1).

The Matter: "How long does Manna last?"

The ABC's of how long Manna lasts in the Torah

Exodus 16:21, 29, 33

Each morning everyone gathered as much as he needed,
and when the sun grew hot, it melted away.

Bear in mind that the LORD has given you the Sabbath,
that is why on the sixth day he gives you bread for two days.

"Take a jar and put an omer of manna in it. Then
place it before the LORD to be kept for generations to come."

The matter defined by the prophet Elijah

I Kings 17:14

For this is what the LORD, the God of Israel, says:
"The jar of flour will not be used up
and the jug of oil will not run dry
until the day the LORD gives rain on the land."

Manna lasts as long as it takes to accomplish God's purpose.

Moses reveals three things about the lasting power of *Manna* in Exodus 16. First, it lasts for one day and requires work to gather it. Second, if necessary, it can last two days if God's purpose needs to be satisfied. The purpose for a two-day supply was God's desire to free man from work that they might spend a day together. Third, it can last forever, if necessary, so all generations may "see" what God fed Israel in the desert. This satisfies a purpose of God. He wants all generations to "see" Him who satisfies the needs of every man. *Manna* lasts as long as it takes to accomplish God's purpose.

Elijah makes this point twice in I Kings 17. First, in verse 1, Elijah said to King Ahab, "As the LORD, the God of Israel, lives, whom I serve, there will be neither dew nor rain in the next few years except at my word." God's purpose in this drought was to reveal Himself as the only true God. "If the LORD is God, follow him; but if Baal is God, follow him."[61] God's Word *(Manna)* causes drought or rain (I Kings 17:1; 18:1-46). It may take *Manna* three years to accomplish God's purpose or it may be done in a day. God's *Manna* stopped the rain for three years while simultaneously feeding Elijah beside the brook in the Cherith Ravine each day.

The second time Elijah makes this point in I Kings 17 is the story of his stay at the home of the widow from Zarephath of Sidon. With only enough flour and oil for a final meal for herself and her son, she first made a cake of bread for Elijah. This was done in obedience to God's Word. "She went away and did as Elijah had told her. So there was food every day for Elijah and for the woman and her family. For the jar of flour was not used up and the jug of oil did not run dry, in keeping with the word of the LORD spoken by Elijah."[62]

What were they eating? *Manna,* perhaps? You see, *Manna* is whatever you need. "My God shall supply all your need according to his riches in glory by Christ Jesus."[63] The Messiah, Jesus, is God's Word. The Word is *Manna. Manna* is the "bread of heaven" so *Manna* is in heaven. Heaven is glory. Glory is filled with riches. God, therefore, supplies all needs with *Manna* stored in glory–His Word–Messiah Jesus! Blessed be He, King of Glory!

Before You Read On!

Take This Exam

1 What do prophets reveal when they preach?
2 Why did Joshua speak so precisely in Joshua 5:10-12?
3 What did Isaiah say God's Word would do?
4 How long does *Manna* last according to Moses and Elijah?
5 What does God use to meet needs?

Read Before Reading Chapter 4

Psalm 78

Nehemiah 9

Psalm 105

Do A Spiritual Exercise

Before you proceed on to Chapter 4, "Manna in the Ketuveem," it would be helpful to log on a piece of paper how many times God has "fed" you *Manna.* Consider just the major events in your life where your "lack" made it impossible for you to take care of the situation yourself.

Manna
in the Ketuveem

"He brought out Israel, laden with silver and gold, and from among their tribes no one faltered. Egypt was glad when they left, because dread of Israel had fallen on them. He spread out a cloud as a covering, and a fire to give them light at night. They asked, and he brought them quail and satisfied them with the bread of heaven. He opened the rock, and water gushed out; like a river it flowed in the desert."

——David (Psalm 105:37-41)

Chapter 4
Manna in the Ketuveem

The Hebrew Bible's (TaNaK) third section of books is called *Ketuveem*. *Ketuveem* is Hebrew for "Writings." The Book of Psalms is the largest Book in the "Writings." It is large because it is actually five "Psalm Books" in one (1-41; 42-72; 73-89; 90-106; 107-150). Because it is so large, the entire third section of the "Writings" is frequently referred to as the "Psalms." Jesus refers to the "Writings" as the "Psalms" in Luke 24:44 where He had earlier (24:27) called this section the "Writings" (Scriptures).

The word *Manna* is used in the *Ketuveem* Book of Psalms in Psalm 78:24. Psalm 78 is a *maskil* (didactic poem) of Asaph written around 1000 B.C. According to I Chronicles 6, 15 and 16, Asaph was "a Levite, son of Berechiah, of the family of Gershom who was eminent as a musician and appointed by [King] David to preside over the sacred choral services."[64] Asaph calls *Manna* both **"the grain of Heaven"** (78:24) and **"the bread of angels."** *Manna* is angel food. Angels eat *Manna*. What did Asaph know about the sustaining power of *Manna?* How long can angels live on *Manna?*

Asaph called *Manna* "the grain (corn) of Heaven" (דְּגַן־שָׁמָיִם *d_egan-sha-ma-yim*). He also called *Manna* "the bread of angels" (אַבִּירִים לֶחֶם *lechem ab-bee-reem*). The Hebrew word in this passage translated "angels" (אַבִּירִים) means "to soar upward in flight."[65] This word includes both orders of biblical angels–Cherubim and Seraphim. Both "fly upward" (Ezk. 10:15 & Isa. 6:2). All Heaven's angels eat *Manna*. All are sustained forever by the Word of God!

The order of biblical angels called Cherubim "are first spoken of as guarding paradise, Gen. 3:24, ..."[66] "After Adam and Eve were driven out of the Garden of Eden, God placed Cherubim and a flaming, revolving sword to guard the road to the tree of life (Gen. 3:24)."[67] According to Isaiah 6:1-7, the Seraphim are "an order of angels attending upon God, and appearing with Him, having six wings."[68] "Saraph" (Hebrew - שָׂרַף) means "to absorb with fire."[69]

"CHERUB The English word, which is a transliteration from Hebrew, ultimately derives from the Akkadian language, in which it refers to an intercessor who brings the prayers of humans to the gods. In the Bible it denotes a winged celestial creature whose prototype is well-known from the art and iconography of the ancient Near East."[70]

Cherubim and Seraphim are both associated with fire in the Bible. "Not only were the Cherubim found in close relationship with the flaming sword when they protected the Garden of Eden, they are said to have walked in the midst of stones of fire in the holy mountain of God (Ezek. 28:14, 16)."[71] Seraphim are six-winged angels who consume with fire. When Isaiah was called to preach, it was a Seraph who took "a live coal in his hand"[72] from God's altar to purge Isaiah's unclean lips. Why must angels be capable of dealing with fire? Because "the LORD your God is a consuming fire!"[73] According to Leviticus chapters 21 and 22, the LORD our God eats with priests and consumes His food with fire! Even the Apostle Paul associates angels with fire at the return to earth of Messiah. He said, "God is just. He will pay back trouble to those who trouble you and give relief to you who are troubled, and to us as well. This will happen when the Lord Jesus is revealed from heaven in blazing fire with his powerful angels."[74]

Manna is the "food" of angels. Cherubim and Seraphim have eaten, are now eating and will forever eat *Manna*. They totally consume (like fire) every Word God speaks. *Manna* is the Word of God. Heaven's grain feeds heaven's beings. Obviously, God's Word (the food of angels) is capable of sustaining life forever. Therefore, mankind must learn that man does not live by the earthly manifestation of heavenly bread alone–but by every Word that comes from the mouth of God.

Angels eat God's Word and obtain all they need. Israelis lived on *Manna* for forty years. All their needs were met. Conclusion? Just like angels, humans can have all their needs met by God's *Manna!* Anyone who receives Jesus as God's Messiah becomes a new, heaven-bound creation. Once assured of a place in heaven, all new creations should change from exclusively devouring an "earth-food" diet and add "angel-food" (the diet of heaven–*Manna).*

Nehemiah

The Book of Nehemiah is found in the *Ketuveem.* It is called Ezra-Nehemiah by the Jews. "The rabbinic authorities (cf. *Bab. Bath.* 15a) regarded the two books as a single composition attributed to Ezra."[75] They were divided around the time of Origen.

"Our only knowledge of Nehemiah comes from the book that bears his name. He was cupbearer to the Persian king, Artaxerxes I (465-425 BC). This was a privileged position. Since there is no mention of his wife, it is likely that he was a eunuch. On receiving news of the desolate state of Jerusalem (probably the result of the events of Ezr. 4:7-23), he obtained permission to go to his own country, and was appointed governor. In spite of intense opposition, he and the Jews rebuilt the walls of Jerusalem in 52 days. He and the other Jews called on Ezra to read the Law, and pledged themselves to observe its commands. During his absence in Persia, some of the abuses that he had put down reappeared, and on his return he had to carry out fresh reforms. His personal memoirs occupy a large part of the Book of Nehemiah, and they reveal him as a man of prayer, action and a devotion to duty."[76]

Nehemiah lived over 900 years after God fed the Israelis *Manna* in the Wilderness. He lived over 500 years after Asaph wrote the *"Manna"* Psalm 78. He lived in captivity in Persia (today's Iran). He was employed in a life-threatening occupation by a foreign, non-kosher king. Nehemiah had every good earthly reason for not knowing about *Manna.* Yet, in Nehemiah chapter nine, he perfectly understands the power-working purpose of *Manna.* How? While serving Artaxerxes, Nehemiah was told about the destruction of Jerusalem. Then, Nehemiah prayed God's Word and asked for favor with the Persian king. God granted that favor. God caused an anti-Jehovah, Persian king to finance Jerusalem's rebuilding and defend the Israeli workmen! God's *Manna* can do all things!

Along with rebuilding Jerusalem, Ezra and Nehemiah desired to obey God's Torah. In fact, it is said of Ezra that he "had devoted himself to the study and observance of the Torah of God, and to teaching its decrees and laws in Israel."[77] This fact made it possible for all to rediscover *Manna.* And, rediscover *Manna* they did!

Remember, proper Bible study starts with the Torah, then the Prophets and then the Writings. The Torah "says it" simply. The Prophets "apply it" correctly based upon Torah. The Writings with their prose and poetry "reveal it" best. Why best? Because, poets, songwriters and historians "say it" best. Their flair for writing reveals truth about Bible subjects hidden in the simpler ABC books of the Torah and Prophets. Nehemiah is a truth-revealing book.

In Nehemiah 9, the Israelis gathered for fasting, wearing sackcloth and putting dust on their heads. They stood and read the Torah for one quarter of the day, then praised the Lord their God.

The Israeli praise of the Lord God under Nehemiah is recorded in Nehemiah 9:5b-37. *First,* they said, "You alone are God" (5b-6). *Second,* they praised God for making a covenant with Abraham who once worshipped idols [Josh. 24:2] (7-8). *Third,* they praised God for making a Name for Himself above all other gods (9-11). *Fourth,* they praised God for making known the Sabbath (13-15). *Fifth,* they praised God for honoring their fathers in spite of their sins (16-21). *Sixth,* they praised God for killing their enemies (22-25). *Seventh,* they praised God for providing for them in spite of their adulterous relationships with other gods (26-27). *Eighth,* they praised God for delivering them in spite of doing "evil in his eyes" [stealing - II Sam. 12:1-10, Psa. 51:3-6] (28). *Ninth,* they praised God for His righteousness and faithfulness even when they bore Him false witness (32-35). *Tenth,* they were able to cry out to the Lord in their distress while coveting what others had (36-37).

The fact that this litany of praise contains 10 distinct sections is worth noting. In fact, the Israeli praise of the Lord God in Nehemiah 9 follows the exact order of the 10 Commandments listed in Exodus 20. The 10 commandments are: *First,* I am God. *Second,* No Graven images. *Third,* Do not take My Name in vain. *Fourth,* Keep the Sabbath Holy. *Fifth,* Honor your father and mother. *Sixth,* Do not kill. *Seventh,* Do not commit adultery. *Eighth,* Do not steal. *Ninth,* Do not bear false witness. *Tenth,* Do not covet.

Obviously, Nehemiah's desire to completely obey God's Torah was revealed when he led the Israeli praise of the Lord God of Israel. He was so committed to precisely obey God's Word that he followed the order of the Ten Commandments while leading this praise! No one can escape the many requests in the Book of Deuteronomy to obey all the commands of the LORD God **and** to walk in all His ways. Nehemiah noticed those requests. Nehemiah read and obeyed Torah. He did God's Word God's way!

Nehemiah mentioned God providing "bread from heaven" (*Manna*) in the Sabbath section of praise (v. 15). This encourages us to believe that God will provide all our needs when we enter His Rest. Isaiah affirms this by saying, "If you keep your feet from breaking the Sabbath and from doing as you please on my holy day, if you call the Sabbath a delight and the LORD's holy day honorable, and if you honor it by not going your own way and not doing as you please or speaking idle words, then you will find your joy in the LORD, and I will cause you to ride on the heights of the land and to feast on the inheritance of your father Jacob. The mouth of the LORD has spoken."[78]

Nehemiah's greatest revelation regarding *Manna* is mentioned in chapter 9 verse 20. Here, Nehemiah links *Manna* with the instruction of God's Holy Spirit. Since *Manna* is God's Word, it is appropriate that it be taught by God's Holy Spirit. Jesus affirmed this when He said, "But the Counselor, the Holy Spirit, whom the Father will send in my name, will **teach you all things** and will remind you of everything I have said to you."[79] John, the disciple whom Jesus loved, also affirmed this by saying, "As for you, the anointing [the Holy Spirit] you have received from him [Jesus] remains in you, and you do not need anyone to teach you. But as his anointing **teaches you** about **all things** and as that anointing is real, not counterfeit–just as it has taught you, remain in him."[80]

Following this national praising of the LORD, the Israeli leaders, Levites and priests wrote a binding agreement. The main clause read, [We will] "follow the Torah of God given through Moses the servant of God and **obey carefully** all the commands, regulations and decrees of the LORD our Lord."[81] The first to put his seal (signature) upon it was *Nehemiah*. To "obey carefully" means to obey God's Word God's way. To do that, one needs the purposeful teaching of God's Holy Spirit because "the letter [of the Torah] kills, but the Spirit gives life."[82] Nehemiah knew the Holy Spirit.

Psalm 105

Like Nehemiah chapter 9, Psalm 105 is a praise offering to the LORD God. Psalm 105:40 says the LORD "satisfied" the descendants of Abraham "with the bread of heaven" (*Manna*). He did so, according to verse 45, "that they might keep his precepts and observe his laws." The point is, God feeds *Manna* to those intending to live out what they eat!

There are several categories of Psalms. There are hymns, laments, thanksgivings, psalms about the "anointed one," and teachings. Psalm 105 falls into the category of "teaching" psalms. These "may also be historical retrospects which either directly or inferentially project the lessons to be derived from the past and which are deemed to be relevant to the occasion of the psalm (Ps. 78, 81, 105, 106, 114)."[83] Note that Psalm 78 and Psalm 105 fall into the same category and are the only two which mention *Manna*. Both convey the same lesson. This lesson, which is always relevant to the current occasion, is that *Manna*-eaters obey God's Word God's way.

"Only 24 psalms have no heading of any sort. Psalms 1, 2, 10, 33, 43, 71, 93-97, 99, 104, 105, 107, 114-119, [135], 136, and 137 may thus be termed "orphan psalms" (Av. Zar. 24b). In each instance, the LXX [Septuagint] repairs the Hebrew deficiency, though in Psalms 105, 107, 114-119, and 135 the addition consists solely of an initial "Hallelujah." In all but Psalms 115 and 118 this term belongs in the Hebrew to the preceding composition."[84]

Nehemiah 9, Psalm 78 and Psalm 105 all rehearse the story of how the LORD God of Israel, the God of Abraham, Isaac and Jacob, provided for His people. They are historical surveys of how the mighty Word of God sustained them through all their "ups and downs." All offer praise to God from those whom God has blessed. Each mentions God's blessing of *Manna*. One cannot help but praise the Living God for His Living *Manna*. It is, after all, the one thing that sustains us all. He is worthy of our praise for having provided us His Word. "In the beginning was the Word, and the Word was with God, and the Word was God. He was with God in the beginning. ... And the Word was made flesh and made his dwelling among us."[85] Jesus is the Word–the *Manna* from heaven.

No wonder Psalm 105 ends with "Hallelujah!" It matters little that the 70 translators of the Hebrew Bible into Greek [Septuagint] placed the "hallelujah" from Psalm 104:35 at the beginning of Psalm 105. Let "hallelujah" be on both ends of this great Psalm! Indeed, praise Jehovah [hallelujah] for all His provision. We join with Asaph, Nehemiah and the author of Psalm 105 by saying "Hallelujah" to the LORD God of Israel for His provision of *Manna*. God's abundant supply of *Manna* is enough for each day. It does supply every need. It is our only source of God's instructions. *Manna* allows man to obey God, God's Way. Jesus **is** the Way (Jn. 14:6).

While Psalm 105 doesn't begin with the words "Psalm of David," it is clear from I Chronicles 16:7 that David committed it "to Asaph and his associates." Because David knew Asaph, David knew about *Manna*. The psalm David committed to Asaph that day recorded in I Chronicles 16:8-22 is Psalm 105:1-15. That which is recorded in I Chronicles 16:23-36 is Psalm 96:1-14. This seems to indicate that David may be the author of both "orphan psalms" 96 and 105.

David, like the great musician and song-writer Asaph, knew the sustaining, life-giving power of God's heavenly *Manna*. He said in Psalm 105:40, "they [the Israelis] asked, and he ... satisfied them with the bread of heaven. He opened the rock, and water gushed out; like a river it flowed in the desert."

Only the bread of heaven can satisfy. Isaiah prophesied that Messiah would "say to the captives, 'Come out,' and to those in darkness, 'Be free!' ... They will neither hunger nor thirst."[86] Jesus said in Matthew 5:6, "Blessed are those who hunger and thirst for righteousness, for they shall be filled." Again, He said in John 6:35, "I am the bread of life. He who comes to me will never go hungry, and he who believes in me will never be thirsty." The song sung about those "who have come out of the great tribulation" recorded in Revelation 8:15-17 says, "They are before the throne of God and serve him day and night in his temple; and he who sits on the throne will spread his tent over them. Never again will they hunger; never again will they thirst. The sun will not beat upon them, nor any scorching heat. For the Lamb at the center of the throne will be their shepherd; he will lead them to springs of living water. And God will wipe away every tear from their eyes."

Before You Read On!

Take This Exam

1 What is *Manna* called in Psalm 78?
2 Who is Asaph?
3 Who is Nehemiah?
4 What is Nehemiah's greatest revelation regarding *Manna?*
5 Who do you think wrote Psalm 105?

Read Before Reading Chapter 5

John 6

John 4:1-42

Matthew 26:17-30

Do A Spiritual Exercise

Before you proceed on to Chapter 5, "Manna in the Gospels," it would be helpful to log on a piece of paper your memories from past communions with the LORD. Note those times when Jesus, the *Manna* from heaven, met your needs by healing you physically, mentally or spiritually.

Manna
in the Gospels

"I am the living bread that came down from heaven. If anyone eats this bread, he will live forever."
——Jesus (John 6:51)

Chapter 5
Manna in the Gospels

The New Testament begins with four Gospel accounts of Jesus Christ. The first three, Matthew, Mark and Luke speak of the humanity of Jesus and are said to be "synoptic" Gospels. This is a Greek word made of two words. "Syn" means "together" and "optic" means "to see." Each story in any of these three Gospels is likely to be recorded in the other two Gospels. Therefore, the same story should be read in all three Gospels and "seen together." The fourth Gospel is John. John's Gospel speaks of the divinity of Jesus. His emphasis is the spiritual truth behind the story recorded.

Jesus said in John 5:39 that the Old Testament "speaks" or "testifies" of Him. Jesus appears as "shadows" in the Old Testament. However, when Jesus was on this earth He was drenched in the full light of the overhead sun! There was no more "dawn of creation," shadow-casting light behind Him from the Torah. There was no more "back lighting" from the Prophets and Writings who began to clarify His shape. Now, in the Gospels, the Old Testament "King-Messiah" could be brought into sharp focus. The Gospels are the "high-noon" record of Who was causing the "shadows" in the Old Testament. The Gospel "light" removes all shadows recorded about Him. Jesus is God's Messiah.

John chapter 6 records Jesus' own words about who He is. Let there be no confusion over Jesus' claim to be the "bread of heaven," the *"Manna"* eaten in the Wilderness or the "He" of "I am He." Jesus' words in John 6 eliminate guesswork and commentary. However, for the sake of comparison to Moses, these pages will highlight some of the light put upon the Living *Manna,* Jesus of Nazereth, who was sent from heaven to earth by God the Father in order to accomplish His eternal purposes.

Moses told the Israelis, "The LORD your God will raise up for you a prophet like me from among your own brothers. You must listen to him."[88] Then, God told Moses, "I will raise up for them a prophet like you from among their brothers; I will put my words in his mouth and he will tell them everything I command him."[89] In Acts 7:37-53, Stephen said, "that prophet" was Jesus.

John chapter 6 is divided into four major sections, all revealing Jesus as *Manna*. Section one is 6:1-15 which recounts Jesus feeding 5,000 men (plus women and children) by using the boy's five barley loaves and two fish. Section two is 6:16-24 which tells of Jesus walking on the water of the Sea of Galilee during a storm to rescue His disciples. Section three is 6:25-59 which is Jesus' discourse about being the bread of heaven, the *Manna* itself, who came down from heaven. Section four is 6:60-71 which records the desertion of many of His disciples because of His *Manna* teachings.

Jesus is the prophet sent by God Who is greater than Moses. Whatever Moses did, prophesied what Jesus would do.

Section One - John 6:1-15 "Just like Moses"

Just like Moses (a Jew), Jesus (a Jew) crossed over to a "far shore" (Gentile side) of the Sea of Galilee and a great crowd followed him because of the miraculous signs he performed. Moses had crossed from the isolation of the Sinai Desert across the "Reed Sea" and following his performance of miraculous signs, a great crowd followed him out of Egypt.

Just like Moses, Jesus went up on a mountain with his disciples just before Passover.

Just like Moses, Jesus had his closest disciples ask, "What will we eat and drink?"

Just like Moses, Jesus fed the multitude (men, women and children) "earthly food" on the Gentile (Egyptian) side of the sea.

Just like Moses, Jesus performed miraculous "signs" to prove He was the Deliverer (Messiah). The Hebrew word translated "sign" is נֵס (neys) and means *"something lifted up, a token to be seen afar off ... metaphorically, a sign, by which any one is warned* (Nu.26:10)."[89] The feeding of the multitude by Jesus is viewed by

Gentile Believers as a miracle. It is viewed by Jewish Believers as a "sign" identifying Jesus as God's Messiah. In fact, the Jewish teacher, Paul, told the Church at Corinth, "Jews demand miraculous signs."[90] The Pharisees said to Jesus, "Teacher, we want to see a miraculous sign from you."[91]

Just like Moses, Jesus dealt with "bread" for the people to eat.

Just like Moses, Jesus revealed that "wages" were not able to buy the necessary bread required by the multitude to eat. You see, the Israelis were held in slavery in Egypt by the Pharaoh (king of Egypt). During that process, they were not paid "wages" for their 39 hard-labor jobs. So, God told Moses to exact the Israeli's wages before their "Exodus" from Egypt (Ex. 3:21-22; 11:1-3; 12:31-42). The point is that even with all this silver, gold and clothing, the Israelis could not purchase bread in the desert!

Just like Moses, Jesus provided enough bread for everyone. This included a full basket for each family of the 12 leader's! Yes, there were 12 tribes. So, there were 12 disciples at this *Manna* feeding.

Just like Moses, Jesus was the choice of the Israelis to become their "Prophet-King."

Section Two - John 6:16-24 "God Delivers"

John 6:16-24 completely fulfilled Exodus chapter 14. Both passages have "terrified" people (Ex. 14:10); the LORD's Presence (a cloud in Ex. 14:20) to protect His people; occurred at night (Ex. 14:20); a "strong wind" (Ex. 14:21); the LORD's power over water preventing it from killing His people (Ex. 14:21-22); and, God's people miraculously crossing the sea (Ex. 14:29). Comparing John 6:16-24 with Exodus 14 is breath-taking! It clearly reveals Jesus as a greater prophet than Moses. Moses, the man who lifted his rod (authority), and, at God's command stretched forth his hand to make the sea part. The hand of Moses represented the hand of God. "You brought your people out of Egypt with signs and wonders, by a mighty hand and an outstretched arm and with great terror."[92] In John 6 (also in Matthew 14:22-36 and Mark 6:45-56), Jesus "is" [seated at] the right Hand of God Whom the water had to obey.

Section Three - John 6:25-59 "Jesus is Manna"

Well, this is the heart of this book. John 6:25-59 is the testimony of Jesus Himself that He is the *Manna*. What Old Testament authors could only prophesy, Jesus now reveals. What Jesus reveals about Himself in John 6, Paul writes to all believers that they may know Jesus as God's *Manna*. Paul said, "Now to him who is able to establish you by my gospel and proclamation of Jesus Christ, according to the revelation of the mystery hidden for long ages past, but now revealed and made known through the prophetic writings by the command of the eternal God, so that all nations might believe and obey him."[93]

In John 6:25-59, Jesus brilliantly and efficiently authenticates the Torah, Prophets and Writings by quoting verses from all three. The Jews asked Jesus for a sign in order for them to believe his statement, "The work of God is this: to believe in the one he has sent."[94] Jesus quoted from the Torah and the Writings, "He gave them bread from heaven to eat" (Exodus 16:4 and Nehemiah 9:15; Psalm 78:24-25) and from the Prophets, "They will be taught from God" (Isaiah 54:13). It is no accident that these are the same *Manna* Bible chapters discussed in this book. Also, the answers Jesus gave about Him being *Manna,* demonstrate that He followed the same "Bible study method" He outlined for Cleopas in Luke 24:27.

"For the bread of God is he" is the first part of John 6:33. This does not say, "For the bread of God is it." *Manna* is a person, not a thing. This is important according to Martin Buber who taught philosophy from 1938 to 1951 at the Hebrew University in Jerusalem. In his book, *I and Thou,* Buber reveals the difference between persons and things. The essence of his book is that two people can relate to each other. However, if there is one person and one thing, only the person can relate to the thing. The thing cannot relate back to the person. Conclusion? Things cannot satisfy. By contrast, "person-to-person" does satisfy because each relates to the other. If *Manna* were only a "piece of bread," a "thing," it could never satisfy. *Manna,* however, is the person Jesus. He relates to us! In fact, He desires such an intimate relationship with us that He offered Himself as bread to be totally consumed by us. Jesus said, "If a man remains in me and I in him, ..." [Wow!] (John 15:5).

Jesus said He is the *Manna*. He said, "I am the **living** bread that came down from heaven."[95] Jesus is that portion of *Manna* that Aaron put in the pot, inside the Ark of the Covenant which was located inside the Holy of Holies! He is the **living** *Manna* for all generations to see. He is that *Manna* which cannot die because He is God's Word. God's Word cannot die. Jesus told His disciples when they asked for signs of His return to earth, "Heaven and earth will pass away, but my words will never pass away."[96] Therefore, Jesus, as *Manna,* said, "For I have come down from heaven not to do my will but to do the will of him who sent me."[97] This statement of Jesus completely fulfills Isaiah 55:11 which says God's Word "will achieve the purpose for which I [God the Father] sent it."

The times and purposes for which Jesus calls Himself Manna
John 6:33
*For the bread of God is he who comes down from heaven
and gives life to the world.*
John 6:35
*I am the bread of life. He who comes to me will never go hungry,
and he who believes in me will never be thirsty.*
John 6:47-48
*I tell you the truth, he who believes has everlasting life.
I am the bread of life.*
John 6:50
*But here is the bread that comes down from heaven,
which a man may eat and not die.*
John 6:51-52
*I am the living bread that came down from heaven.
If anyone eats of this bread, he will live forever.
This bread is my flesh, which I will give for the life of the world.*
John 6:53-58
*I tell you the truth, unless you eat the flesh of the Son of Man
and drink his blood, you have no life in you.
Whoever eats my flesh and drinks my blood has eternal life,
and I will raise him up at the last day.
For my flesh is real food and my blood is real drink.
Whoever eats my flesh and drinks my blood remains in me,
and I in him. Just as the living Father sent me and I live
because of the Father, so the one who feeds on me will live
because of me. This is the bread that came down from heaven.*

Manna-eaters live forever! Therefore, Jesus can never die since He is the living *Manna*. It follows then that those who abide in Him can never die.

Section Four - John 6:60-71 "Words of Life"

The subject of "Who is the *Manna?*" is the line of demarcation. There is nothing ambiguous here. According to Jesus, if you eat *Manna* you live–if you don't eat *Manna* you die. You either believe Jesus and therefore follow His words or you do not believe Jesus and therefore do not follow His words. Jesus either is or is not *Manna*. The decision about this is a life or death matter. In this passage some followed Jesus because He alone had the "words of eternal life" (v. 68) but "many of his disciples turned back and no longer followed him" (v. 66). Both groups were individuals who made a decision. A decision about Who Jesus is must be made by every human being. Some decided to accept Jesus. Others decided to reject Jesus. The question still remains. Is Jesus God's Messiah?

All who accept Jesus as God's Messiah, *Manna* sent from heaven to give life to all who will eat it, must make a confession. That confession is: "Thou art the Christ, the Son of the living God."[98] It is Peter who makes this bold claim. He repeats this same claim at Caesarea Philippi when Jesus asked His disciples, "Who do you say I am?" (Matt. 16:15-16) The Hebrew text reveals a depth of understanding of who Jesus really is in these two New Testament passages. They read, אַתָּה הוּא הַמָּשִׁיחַ בֶּן־אֱלֹהִים חַיִּים: (atta hu ha-mashiach ben elohim chay-yeem). Literally translated, "You (are) He, the Messiah, [natural born] Son of the Living God." According to Paul, this confession must be made with the mouth and believed in the heart (Rom. 10:9-10). This is why Peter spoke the confession with his mouth (John 6:69) and also told Jesus, "We believe and are sure" (in their hearts) that you, Jesus, are He–Man Hu.

Further proof that Jesus had accomplished His Father's purpose was His ascension back into heaven. Jesus asked His disciples, "What if you see the Son of Man ascend to where he was before?"[99] These same disciples did see Jesus ascend (Acts 1:9) in a cloud. A cloud is the proof that it has rained, the rain water did its work in the earth and has now ascended back to heaven where it all began.

Matthew 26:26-28

During His final Passover meal with His disciples, Jesus clearly identified the piece of *Matza* bread (known as the 'afikomen' - dessert in Greek) that had been hidden during the meal as "My Body." He blessed God for the bread by saying, "Baruch atta Adonai Elohenu Melek HaOlam, ha-motzi lechem min ha-aretz" (Blessed art Thou O LORD our God Who brings forth bread from the earth). Jesus was prophesying about His resurrection in the blessing.

In verse 26 He told His disciples, "Take and eat, this is my body." In I Corinthians 11:24, Paul said Jesus asked us to eat the bread "in remembrance of me." Each communion presents an opportunity to remember what Jesus, the bread that came down from heaven to accomplish God's will, has done for us. This is why the bread should not be eaten "unworthily" (I Cor. 11:27). Self-examination is for the purpose of not eating unworthily. That is, each communicant should ascribe to the Bread of Heaven His worth before eating!

John 4:27-38

Jesus and His disciples went through the region known as Samaria to a town called Sychar (Old Testament Shechem, Nablus today). While there, Jesus went to the town well. His disciples went to town to buy food. At the well, Jesus met and spoke with a Samaritan woman. The disciples returned to the well and were upset when they found Jesus talking with the woman. They "urged" him to eat. Jesus' answer reveals that he had been eating and serving *Manna*.

Jesus answered His disciples in John 4:32, "I have food to eat that you know nothing about." You see, when one is carrying out His will, the Father provides all that is needed. The "food" Jesus spoke of was obviously *Manna*. *Manna* does the will of the Father. That is why Jesus answered his foolish disciples (who thought someone else had brought Jesus earthly food), "My food is to do the will of him who sent me and to finish his work" (John 4:34). It is also obvious why Jesus used this situation to make His appeal for believers to join Him in the harvest. As with Jesus, God provides harvesters all they need to help Him bring in the harvest of souls— souls like this half-breed, divorced, outcast woman at the well.

Before You Read On!

Take This Exam

1 In John 6, how many ways is Jesus "just like Moses?"
2 Who does Jesus claim to be in John 6:25-59?
3 Why don't "Manna-eaters" ever die?
4 What is the confession that must be made with the mouth
  and believed in the heart if one wants eternal life?
5 What other food did Jesus have while in Sychar?

Read Before Reading Chapter 6

I Corinthians 10

Hebrews 9

Philippians 4:10-20

Do A Spiritual Exercise

Before you proceed on to Chapter 6, "Manna in the
Epistles," make a prayer list of individuals that need to receive Jesus Christ as LORD of their lives. As you read this
6th chapter, make notes alongside each person's name on
your list as the Holy Spirit speaks to you regarding them.

Manna
in the Epistles

"For I have learned to be content whatever the circumstances. I know what it is to be in need, and I know what it is to have plenty. I have learned the secret of being content in any and every situation, whether well fed or hungry."

——**Paul** (Phil. 4:11-12)

Chapter 6
Manna in the Epistles

The second main section of the New Testament is considered "The Epistles" (The Letters). Although generally said to be a book of history, the Book of Acts should be thought of as the "Living Epistle." That is, Acts is the book in the New Testament which records the places Jesus' Apostles visited, started congregations and then later wrote "epistles." The "Epistles" to congregations include Romans, I Corinthians, II Corinthians, Galatians, Ephesians, Philippians, Colossians, I Thessalonians, II Thessalonians and Hebrews. The "Epistles" to Church leaders include I Timothy, II Timothy, Titus, I Peter, II Peter, I John, II John and III John. The general "Epistles" are Philemon, James and Jude.

All apostolic letters were written to congregations and individuals who believed that Jesus was God's Messiah. Members of these congregations were both Jews and Gentiles. This meant that some from each congregation had little or no knowledge of the Old Testament. Often, they were from polytheistic (belief in many gods) backgrounds. The "pagan" members of these Messianic congregations needed accurate Bible instruction concerning the Jewish background of their newly found Messiah, Jesus.

The Old Testament contains "shadows" of Messiah. The Gospels shed brilliant light upon Jesus identifying Him as God's Messiah. The "Epistles" explain to both Jews and Gentiles within the Church how the Jesus of the Gospels fulfilled Messianic passages from the Old Testament. As an added note, the Epistles are sometimes called "problem literature" because they were written to solve "problems" within the Jewish/Gentile congregations.

The facts mentioned above make one ask, "Which 'Epistles' (and other books) should be included in the body of literature commonly called the New Testament?" Since Jesus is God's Messiah, which "New Covenant" Epistles, Gospels or other books, ought to be included to correctly identify Him as such?

Canonization

The process of selecting books to be included in the New Testament (and Old Testament) is called canonization. The Greek word κανών (kanon) means "straight, level or rule."[100] Also, "there is no denying that the OT was regarded as Scripture by the Christian Church. It may be safely assumed that the Christians regarded the OT as inspired, in common with the Jews from whom they took over these Scriptures. Since the earliest Christians were Jewish, this would be expected. Moreover, there can be no doubt that Jesus shared the same view [Luke 24:27] of the inspiration of the OT. The concept of an authoritative collection of sacred books was therefore provided before any of the New Testament books were written."[101] Some of the major standards by which an "Epistle" would be accepted in the New Testament canon were: 1) written by an Apostle or "eye-witness" of Jesus; 2) suitable for public reading; 3) obviously inspired by God's Holy Spirit; and, 4) that it accurately quoted from the Old Testament.

Paul's First Letter to the Church at Corinth

Paul's first letter to the Church at Corinth is commonly called I Corinthians. The Church at Corinth, Greece, was deficient in "spiritual maturity and moral stability."[102] Corinth was a city rebuilt for human pleasures by the Roman emperors. It was a city divided between those with great wealth and the servants who worked for them. It was a center for the worship of Greek and Roman gods. As a result, this was a church with a clear deficiency regarding spiritual matters. In spite of this, in I Corinthians "Paul singled out those features [within this church] for which he could sincerely thank God, and be assured that, as they waited for the revelation of Christ [Messiah] at His parousia [return appearance], they could rely for their establishment on their faithful God, who has called them into the fellowship of His Son (I Cor. 1:1-9)."[103]

The "revelation" that Jesus is God's Messiah is highlighted by Paul's words found in I Corinthians 10:1-10. This compact portion of Scripture addresses who Jesus is and appeals to the new Corinthian converts not to continue their worship of idols. Paul told them that Old Testament stories were "examples" to keep them pure of heart.

Chief among the Old Testament "example" stories chosen by Paul is the Exodus account of *Manna.* Paul called the *Manna* eaten by the Israelis in the Sinai desert "spiritual food" (I Cor. 10:3). He used this term to contrast it with food offered to idols in an earlier discourse (I Cor. 8). They are not the same. One is earthly food offered by man to a "so-called god."[104] The other, *Manna,* is heavenly food offered to man by the only "one God, the Father, from whom all things came and for whom we live; and there is but one Lord, Jesus Christ, through whom all things come and through whom we live."[105] *Manna* is "spiritual food" for the spiritual man.

Paul used the Exodus story to remove ignorance in the new Believers regarding: 1) water baptism; 2) Christ is the Believer's spiritual food and drink; 3) the wrath of God; 4) idolatry; 5) sexual immorality; 6) not to test the Lord; and, 7) not to grumble against God's provision. It is impressive to give all this teaching in just 10 verses. But, the core message in this passage was that Jesus is God's Messiah. Also, consider that when Paul wrote this corrective letter to the Corinthian Church, there was no New Testament. Using *Manna* as an "example," he taught that Jesus is Messiah exclusively from the Old Testament. His preaching from the Old Testament about Jesus being Messiah removed, for all time, the "ignorance" in both Jewish and Gentile Believers concerning this issue.

Earlier in this Epistle, Paul discussed the difference between the "natural" man and the "spiritual" man. He said, "The natural man receiveth not the things of the Spirit of God: for they are foolishness unto him: neither can he know *them,* because they are spiritually discerned."[106] When the "natural" man hears spiritual truth it passes through him like a sieve. He is unable to retain it. By contrast, the "spiritual" man, who requires spiritual food, not only retains it–he grows by it. Paul told the Believers in Colossae, "So then, just as you received Christ Jesus as Lord, continue to live in him, rooted and built up in him, strengthened in the faith as you were taught, and overflowing with thankfulness."[107] The "spiritual food" (*Manna*) required by the spiritual man is Christ–God's Word. *Manna* tastes like honey (Exodus 16:31; Psalm 19:10) and strengthens the inner man. Paul prayed for the Believers at Ephesus (3:16). He said, "I pray that out of his glorious riches he may strengthen you with power by his Spirit in your inner being." LORD, may it be!

Hebrews 9:1-15

The author of the Book of Hebrews is not identified within the Book itself. "In spite of traditional ascriptions and brilliant guesses, its authorship is unknown. At Alexandria [Egypt] it was ascribed to Paul from the second half of the 2nd century onward, although difficulties in this ascription were acknowledged by Clement and Origen: "God knows the truth of the matter," said the latter (Euseb. Hist. vi. 25.14). Tertullian ascribed it to Barnabas (*De pudicitia* 20). Luther's ascription to Apollos has commended itself to many; Harnack's ascription to Priscilla seems to be ruled out by the masculine participle in Hebrews 11:32. The author was a second generation Christian master of a fine literary style, quite unlike Paul's; like Apollos, he may have had an Alexandrian Jewish background and he was certainly "well versed in the scriptures," which he knew in the LXX VS and interpreted according to a creative exegetical principle."[108]

Hebrews 9:1-5 describes the structure called the Tabernacle of Moses (Ex. 26; 36). It identifies the two separate rooms–The Holy Place and The Most Holy Place–called in Exodus "The Holy Place" and "The Holy of Holies." Hebrews 9:3 calls the "Veil" (Ex. 26:33) that separated the two rooms the "second curtain."

The author of Hebrews makes a brilliant observation regarding the furnishings within the two rooms. He said the Most Holy Place contained "the golden altar of incense and the gold-covered ark of the covenant." He chooses to explain Exodus 25 and 26:31-35 with Exodus 30:1-5 in the light of Jesus, God's *Manna*. You see, the "altar of incense" is described in Exodus 30 not in Exodus 25. Some scholars consider its description "out of place." Other scholars have noticed that the "altar of incense" is not mentioned in Leviticus 16–the chapter regarding the Day of Atonement service. Neither is it mentioned in Solomon's Temple (I Kings 6) or the Messianic Temple prophesied by Ezekiel (Ezekiel 40ff.). All scholars place the "golden altar of incense" in "front" of the veil separating the two rooms. Yet, the author of Hebrews places the altar of incense "inside" the Holy of Holies right beside the ark of the covenant. Is this Jewish author and believer in Jesus as Messiah in error? Where does the altar of incense belong–and when?

Hebrews 9:1-5 puts the focus on the furnishings, not the rooms. Interestingly, "The Torah describes the furniture before it depicts the structure of the shrine, because the 'vessels' were considered the more important; the Tabernacle and court merely housed them."[109]

The focus should be on the "vessels." All of the furnishings of the Tabernacle of Moses are "types" of Messiah. The Messiah is every vessel!

How could the author of Hebrews describe the vessel, the altar of incense, as being **in** the Holy of Holies beside the ark of the covenant? Is he mistaken? No! They are both in the same room because the veil which separated them had been removed! That "second curtain" is the body of Jesus, the Messiah (Heb. 10:20). Its removal, by the death of Jesus (Matt. 27:51), has given us all (as altars of incense) access into the very Presence of God (Heb. 10:19).

As described in Exodus 30:1-10, the altar of incense was used twice daily by Aaron to burn fragrant incense before the LORD God. It was mandated to continue throughout all generations. All other daily offerings were forbidden. Only fragrant incense could be put upon the altar of incense. Except, "Once a year Aaron shall make atonement on its horns. This annual atonement must be made with the blood of the atoning sin offering [lamb of God] for the generations to come. It must be holy to the LORD."[110]

Jesus Christ, the veil separating the Holy Place from the Holy of Holies, has given Himself for all (whose lives are to also be a "sweet-smelling" sacrifice) to enter into God's Presence. "Be imitators of God, therefore, as dearly loved children and live a life of love, just as Christ loved us and gave himself up for us as a fragrant offering and sacrifice to God (Eph. 5:2)." Jesus is the altar of incense. He gave Himself to God daily as an incense offering, pleasing to God. He also gave Himself as a sacrifice to God once and for all time as the blood sacrifice for all generations to come.

Believers are likened unto the altar of incense as well. They, too, may enter into God's Presence. Hebrews 10:22 gives permission to all Believers to enter His Presence because they, like the altar of incense, have been "sprinkled and washed" by the blood of the Lamb.

Hebrews 9:4 says the ark of the covenant "contained the gold jar of manna." The *Manna* in the gold jar was the "living" *Manna*. It was the *Manna* for all generations to see. It was the *Manna* placed in front of the ark of the covenant by Aaron as instructed by Moses (Ex. 16:33-35). According to the author of Hebrews, that same *Manna* is no longer outside the ark, He is inside the ark! Who placed Him inside the ark? The LORD Himself! The "living" bread is now ready for all believers to eat for all eternity. Blessed be He!

Philippians 4:10-20

This wonderful letter to the Church at Philippi contains full disclosure as to the identity of Jesus. Here, in Philippians 2:6 (KJV), Paul identifies Jesus as "equal with God." God and God's Word are inseparable. They are the "same." The Hebrew word for "same" is אֶחָד (echad). This word "echad" is found in the twice-daily recitation of praise to God known as the *"Shema"* (Deut. 6:4-9). Deuteronomy 6:4 says, "Hear, O Israel: the LORD our God, the LORD is one (echad)."

You will notice the word "LORD" is used twice in Deuteronomy 6:4. Since Israel is being asked to "hear," it follows that they are to "hear" God's Word. The first "LORD" in this verse represents God the Father. It is confirmed by being first in the verse and by the identifier "the LORD our God." According to Exodus 20:1-2, the Jews can have no other God before the LORD, not even His Word! This is illustrated on the doorpost of every Jewish home. On their doorposts, even the *"Mezuzah"* leans. The *Mezuzah* (translated "doorpost" Deut. 6:9) is a box containing God's Word. The other "LORD" represents God the Word. This is not a redundant use of God's Name. It is a demonstration of the Holy Spirit that God and His Word are inseparable. Yes Paul, Jesus is "equal with God."

In Philippians 4:10-20, Paul described how *Manna* supplied his needs through the hands of the believers at Philippi. This passage contains two of the most frequently quoted verses in the Bible. The first is 4:13 which says, *"I can do all things through Christ which strengtheneth me"* (KJV). The second is 4:19 which says, *"But my God shall supply all your need according to his riches in glory by Christ Jesus"* (KJV). Both verses are all about *Manna*.

Philippians 4:13 indicates that Christ (*Manna*) "strengthens" men to enable them to do "all things." *Manna* is not only "tasty" (like honey), it is "nutritious." *Manna* is like rain and snow (Isa. 55) that waters seed for growth. Plants that grow as the result of having received rain and snow (*Manna*) provide next year's seed for sowing and this year's bread for eaters! *Manna* "strengthens" plants into this useful maturity. Likewise, when consumed daily (Psa. 1), *Manna* makes a man "prosper." *Manna*-eaters' leaves do not "wither" and they always "produce fruit in season."

Digested *Manna* strengthens men's hearts for new and great possibilities. Its very "living" Presence encourages men to do impossible things. *Manna* releases the **"I can do"** inside a man. Walter Matthews said, "First we think, then we act. To consciously think that we "can" impels the subconscious faculties into action" (*Distilled Wisdom,* Prentice Hall, Inc., Englewood Cliffs, N.J., p. 320). **"I can do all things"** is either the most arrogant statement anyone can make, or, it is the direct result of the unleashed power of *Manna* inside a man. Since it comes from the Word Himself ("I can do all things through Christ which strengtheneth me"), it is not a statement of arrogance–it is a statement of fact! *Manna* strengthens all who eat Him in order to enable them to do all things.

Philippians 4:19 is the promise of God to fulfill Philippians 4:13. Since *Manna* strengthens to enable, it is up to God to supply Himself as *Manna*. Both men and angels are dependent upon *Manna* for their sustenance. Both would die without *Manna*. Both will live forever because they both eat *Manna* daily.

The Apostle Paul confirms that *Manna* comes from heaven. Like Asaph in Psalm 78:25, Paul states that "God will supply all your need according to his riches in glory." *Manna* is the bread of heaven (glory). It can become whatever is needed on earth.

In Philippians 4:19, the word "need" is in the singular. The reason is simple. Whatever you need, God says, "I am." Since God is "One" so is man's need. Also, "By Christ Jesus" indicates that Christ Jesus is the vessel through which God supplies man's need. He is the "ladder" which connects heaven to earth for transporting *Manna* as seen by Jacob (Genesis 28:12) and by Nathaniel (John 1:51).

Before You Read On!

Take This Exam

1 What do the Epistles explain about Jesus?
2 What makes the natural and spiritual man different?
3 Who wrote the Book of Hebrews?
4 Where did the author of the Book of Hebrews locate the altar of incense?
5 Who is equal with God?

Read Before Reading Chapter 7

Revelation 2:12-17

Matthew 3:13-4:11

Revelation 20

Do A Spiritual Exercise

Before you proceed on to Chapter 7, "Manna in the Revelation," it would be helpful to log on a piece of paper how many times and ways you have been tempted to do wrong. Keep this sheet of paper until you have read chapter 7 and then find verses that offer victory over each temptation.

Manna
in the Revelation

"To him who overcomes, I will give some of the hidden manna."
——Jesus (Rev. 2:17)

Chapter 7
Manna in the Revelation

Jesus is revealed in the Book of Revelation. Sound redundant? No, this double emphasis is made here in order that Bible students grasp the relevance of this Book. The first line of this book says, "The Revelation of Jesus Christ." Many have tried to make this prophecy other things. However, one thing is clear from its author–God's Holy Spirit–it is the revelation of Jesus Christ.

Jesus, the Bread of Heaven, is revealed in Revelation. It is as simple as A, B, C. This Book contains 22 chapters. There are 22 letters in the Hebrew alphabet. So, Revelation might be like an acrostic of the Hebrew alphabet. For example, Jesus is revealed as the "Aleph" (alpha in Greek) in Revelation chapter 1 and the "Tau" (omega in Greek) in chapter 22. Also, He affirms Himself as the "door" (4th Hebrew letter–Daleth [door]) in chapter 4:1, the "hand" (10th Hebrew letter–Yodh [hand]) in chapter 10:2 and the "sign" (15th Hebrew letter–Samech [signet]) in chapter 15:1.

How does He reveal Himself as *Manna* in the Revelation?

In Chapter 2:12-17, He spoke to the church in Pergamum. He asked them to repent from: 1) eating food offered to idols; 2) committing sexual immorality; and, 3) the teaching of the Nicolations. "Ireaneus said that they were followers of Nicolaus of Antioch, a proselyte who was among the seven men chosen to serve the Jerusalem congregation (Acts 6:5), who ... lived in unrestrained indulgence."[111]

According to Jesus in Revelation 2:14, these false and abhorrent doctrines were part of the "seduction" of Balaam to the Israelis (Numbers 25:1-5 with Numbers 31:16). According to Jesus, like Israel before them, the Pergamum church had been "seduced" by Nicolaus into the same lifestyle. These sins are forbidden at the Council in Jerusalem in Acts 15:28-29. Who was behind both seductions? Satan! Satan, whose throne (2:13) was in their city!

Satan is real. Satan is God's enemy. Accordingly, Satan attacks God's army–God's people. Satan's method of attacking God's people is to steal God's Word from them. Jesus said, "Satan comes and takes away the word [*Manna*] that was sown in them."[112] Paul says that Satan is capable of "outwitting" people with his "schemes."[113] Satan's overall objective is to impose his will above God's. He does this by pitting humans against God. In his encouragement to young Timothy, Paul warned him by saying, "And the Lord's servant must not quarrel, instead, he must be kind to everyone, able to teach, not resentful. Those who oppose him he must gently instruct, in the hope that God will grant them repentance leading them to a knowledge of the truth, and they will come to their senses and escape from the trap of the devil, who has taken them captive to do his will."[114] Jesus appeared to destroy this work of Satan (I Jn. 3:8).

"Satan" is actually the title for the cherub-order angel named Lucifer. Isaiah (14:12) identified Lucifer, his status and his plan of attacking God. He said, "How art thou fallen from heaven, O Lucifer, son of the morning! *How* art thou cut down to the ground, which did weaken the nations!" John identified Lucifer as "The great dragon [who] was hurled down–that ancient serpent called the devil, or Satan, who leads the whole world astray. He was hurled to the earth, and his angels with him."[115] Ezekiel also identified Lucifier:

"You were the model of perfection, full of wisdom and perfect in beauty. You were in Eden, the garden of God, every precious stone adorned you, ruby, topaz and emerald, chrysolite, onyx and jasper, sapphire, turquoise and beryl. Your settings and mountings were made of gold, on the day you were created they were prepared. You were anointed as a guardian cherub for so I ordained you. You were on the holy mount of God; you walked among the fiery stones. You were blameless in your ways from the day you were created till wickedness was found in you. Through your widespread trade you were filled with violence, and you sinned. So I drove you in disgrace from the mount of God, and I expelled you, O guardian cherub, from among the fiery stones. Your heart became proud on account of your beauty, and you corrupted your wisdom because of your splendor. So I threw you to the earth, I made a spectacle of you before kings. By

your many sins and dishonest trade you have desecrated your sanctuaries. So I made a fire come out from you, and it consumed you, and I reduced you to ashes on the ground in sight of all who were watching. All the nations who knew you are appalled at you, you have come to a horrible end and will be no more." Ezekiel 28:12-19

According to Ezekiel, Satan was adorned with precious stones. These are the same precious stones identifying the sons of Israel and worn on the breastpiece of Israel's High Priest. That is, all except three of them. There was **ruby** (Reuben - 1st born by Leah); **topaz** (Simeon - 2nd born by Leah); **emerald** (Napthali - 6th born by Bilhah); **chrysolite** (Zebulun - 10th born by Leah); **onyx** (Joseph - 11th born by Rachel); **jasper** (Benjamin - 12th born by Rachel); **sapphire** (Dan - 5th born by Bilhah); **turquoise** (Judah - 4th born by Leah); and, **beryl** (Levi - 3rd born by Leah). The three stones not mentioned are: **jacinth** (Gad - 7th born by Zilpah); **agate** (Asher - 8th born by Zilpah) and, **amethyst** (Issachar - 9th born by Leah). Why might the stones of Jacob's seventh, eighth and ninth sons be missing?

One thing these three sons may have in common is found in the blessing of Moses over the tribes recorded in Deuteronomy chapter 33. Moses said to Gad in verse 21, "When the heads of the people assembled, he [Gad] carried out the LORD's righteous will, and his judgments concerning Israel." Moses said to Asher in verse 24, "Most blessed of sons is Asher." Moses said to Issahcar in verse 19, "They [Issachar] will summon peoples to the mountain and there offer sacrifices of righteousness." All three were blessed with a thirst and hunger for righteousness. Satan cannot defeat those who are "filled" with the righteousness of God.

Ezekiel twice identifies Satan as a "guardian cherub" (Ez. 28:14, 16). In chapter 4 of this book, "Manna in the Ketuveem," page 44, there is information concerning the order of angels called cherubim. Ezekiel calls Satan a "cherub" who walked among "fiery stones." An attribute of angels is that they are associated with fire. It is more than interesting that God "made a fire come out of Satan" and that fire consumed Satan. This is exactly Satan's end as described by John in Revelation 20:7-10.

Satan's fiery end is assured. It is what he is capable of doing to men until his end comes that is concerning. His attacks are increasing. His problem according to John is time. "But woe to the earth and the sea, because the devil has gone down to you! He is filled with fury, because he knows his time is short!"[116] Satan has very little time left to steal, kill and destroy!

Satan, as a cherub angel, had to have eaten the angel food of heaven. When God cast him down to the earth, Satan, among other things, lost his ability to eat *Manna* directly. What once fed Satan now destroys him–God's Word. John said he heard a loud voice from heaven say, "Now have come the salvation and the power and the kingdom of our God, and the authority of his Christ. For the accuser of our brothers [Satan], who accuses them before our God day and night [Job 1:6-12; 2:1-8], has been hurled down. They [brothers] overcame him [Satan] by the blood of the Lamb and by the word [*Manna*] of their testimony."[117] In the end, God's Word defeats Satan (Rev. 19:17-21). God's Word always defeats Satan. "When evening came, many who were demon-possessed were brought to him [Jesus], and he drove out the spirits with a word."[118]

Satan's destruction and Believers' salvation are indicated in the prophecy about *Manna* given by Moses. Remember from chapter 2 of this book, "Manna in the Torah," page 24, it quotes Deuteronomy 8:16 which says *Manna* was given "to humble and to test you [Israel] so that in the end it might go well with you." Those who eat *Manna* receive eternal life. They do not die along with Satan. "In the end," it goes well with *Manna*-eaters! Hallelujah! The LORD "will swallow up death forever."[119]

Satan knows his end. Satan knows about life without *Manna*. He knows that only *Manna*-eaters survive. Why do you suppose he doesn't want humans to eat *Manna?* You know, humans, those who sinned against God just as Satan did. Humans, who, if they accept God's *Manna* as the full payment for their sins, receive a pardon from the penalty of their sins and eternal life as their reward! Satan sinned and was "expelled" from heaven. Satan had no chance at redemption (Rev. 20:7-10). Satan sinned and was lost forever. Man sinned, yet he can be saved forever if he eats *Manna*. No wonder angels desire (I Peter 1:12) to look into this matter!

The Hebrew word for "Satan" is שָׂטָן (transliterally - "satan"). It means *"lier in wait, adversary ...* as in war, *enemy, ...* the evil genius ... who seduces men (1 Chron. 21:1)."[120] "Satan" means "trapsetter." When Solomon confessed the LORD with his mouth and trusted Him with his heart (Psa. 91:2), his father, David said that the LORD would first of all "deliver him from the snare" of Satan, the fowler (Psa. 91:3). There is power over Satan's temptations when one speaks and obeys God's Word.

Nowhere is it made more clear that Satan is overcome by God's Word than the story recounting Jesus' 40-day fast in the wilderness. Following His baptism by John, "Jesus was led by the Spirit into the desert to be tempted by the devil."[121] Satan does his best to attempt to gain superiority over God's Word. God's Word had "expelled" Satan to his own destruction. Now Satan has come face to face with God's Word. They are together in the desert with no one else around. The battle scene is set. Can God's *Manna* utterly defeat God's enemy? We shall look at Matthew 4:1-11 to see.

Satan's first temptation for Jesus was aimed at Jesus' flesh. Since Jesus had not eaten for forty days, He was hungry. Thinking he had an advantage over Jesus in the flesh, Satan said (v. 3) "If you are the Son of God, tell these stones to become bread." Satan knew that whatever God's Word would say had to happen. Yet, Jesus, God's Word, did not command the stones to become bread. That would have made Jesus submit to the word of Satan. Instead, Jesus rebuked Satan (v. 4), "It is written: 'Man does not live on bread alone, but on every word that comes from the mouth of God.'" Round one of Jesus versus Satan in the flesh went to Jesus! He overcame Satan's temptation of the flesh by knowing and acting upon God's Word.

Satan's second temptation for Jesus was aimed at Jesus' mind. Having failed to defeat Jesus in the flesh, Satan tried a mind game with Jesus. Also, since Jesus quoted a Scripture to defeat him, Satan now tried to tempt Jesus by "mis"quoting an application of Scripture. Furthermore, Satan quoted a Scripture out of context from Psalm 91–the very Scripture that prophesys his defeat! Satan tempts Jesus to "throw himself down" from the highest point of the Temple. He quotes Scripture (Ps. 91:11-12) to Jesus. Imagine the audacity of quoting Scripture to the Word Himself. Jesus defeated Satan by obeying God's Word. Jesus won round two–the "mind game" against Satan–by answering, "It is also written: 'Do not put the LORD your God to the test'" (Deut. 6:16).

Satan's third temptation for Jesus was aimed at Jesus' spirit. Satan (v. 8-9) took Jesus to a very high mountain and said to Him, "All of this I will give you if you bow down and worship me." Jesus won round three–the battle for spiritual authority–by quoting Deut. 6:13, "Worship the LORD your God, and serve him only."

Jesus overcame Satan's physical, mental and spiritual temptations by acting upon God's Word [*Manna*]. This same overcoming power was promised by Jesus to the Pergamum Church in Revelation 2:17. He said to them, "To him who overcomes [Satan], I will give some of the hidden manna." This is not future tense "will give." It is present tense "will give." Whosoever wishes to overcome Satan with God's Word, Jesus will give them "hidden manna."

The Greek word δώσω (doso) is translated here "will give." As used here, it is in the "1st person, singular, future tense, indicative mood and active"[122] voice. What this means is that "from now on," anytime you wish to defeat Satan, I, Jesus, "will give" you the weapon–*Manna*–which will defeat all his attacks against you physically, mentally and spiritually! "(For the weapons of our warfare *are* not carnal, but mighty through God to the pulling down of strongholds;) Casting down imaginations, and every high thing that exalteth itself against the knowledge of God, and bringing into captivity every thought to the obedience of Christ."[123] "When the enemy shall come in, like a flood the Spirit of the LORD shall lift up a standard against him."[124] *Manna* defeats Satan even though he goes about "like a roaring lion, seeking [*Manna*-eaters] to devour."[125]

Be comforted by the Apostle Jesus loved. John said, "Every spirit that acknowledges that Jesus Christ has come in the flesh is from God, but every spirit that does not acknowledge Jesus is not from God. This is the spirit of Antichrist, which you have heard is coming and now is already in the world. You, dear children, are from God and have overcome them, because the one who is in you is greater than the one who is in the world."[126]

Manna in the Torah helped establish the nation of Israel.

Manna in the Nevieem accomplishes God's purposes.

Manna in the Ketuveem restored the nation of Israel.

Manna in the Gospels gives eternal life to all who believe.

Manna in the Epistles feeds the spiritual man.

Manna in the Revelation defeats our enemy–Satan.

What can He do for you? _Manna_ is God's Word. _Manna_ is every Word that came from or will ever come from God's mouth. Man does not live by earthly bread alone. He was created to live forever on heavenly bread, _Manna_–the food of angels.

In these last days, it is critical for believers in Messiah Jesus to help themselves to a daily diet of _Manna_. There are many morsels which are necessary for spiritual growth that are hidden in the depths of God's Word. They need to be found and eaten to bring new life. His Spirit is calling people to do just that–study His Word. They are being called from all over the earth and in every language to study the Bible. In light of this, my request to you is Paul's request to Timothy. It is, "Do your best to present yourself to God as one approved, a workman who does not need to be ashamed and who correctly handles the word of truth."[127]

As a teacher, I realize that studying is hard work. Solomon, who asked for wisdom rather than money and political power, is the wisest man who has ever lived. About study he said, "Much study wearies the body."[128] However, Hosea issued God's warning about not studying. He wrote, "My people are destroyed from lack of knowledge."[129] Also, Paul warned against believers who were "always learning but never able to acknowledge the truth."[130] By contrast, "To the Jews who had believed him, Jesus said, 'If you hold to my teaching, you are really my disciples. Then you will know the truth, and the truth will set you free ... If the Son sets you free, you will be free indeed.'"[131]

אמן ואמן (Amen & Amen)

The Book Has Been Read!

So, Take This Final Exam

1 Who does the Book of Revelation reveal?
2 What type of angel is Satan?
3 What does Lucifer's title, "Satan," mean?
4 How, and, in what three areas did Jesus defeat Satan while fasting in the desert?
5 What does Jesus give those wanting to defeat Satan?

Read After Reading Chapter 7

Psalm 91

Ephesians 6:10-18

Epilogue

Do A Spiritual Exercise

Having read these 7 chapters on "Manna," it would be helpful to log on the piece of paper you wrote at the end of chapter 6 all the Bible verses that defeat your temptations from Satan. There may be more than one verse that overcomes each temptation. Happy digging! Happy eating!

Epilogue

There is a purpose to everything under the sun. What is the purpose of this book? Since I desire to overcome the temptations presented by Satan when I am alone, I assume other believers in Yeshua desire the same. I have discovered that only when I am a "doer " of God's Word *(Manna)* do I overcome Satan's temptations. So, I just wanted to pass that discovery along to other Pilgrims seeking similar victories in their lives.

Satan has robbed *Manna* from Believers in Yeshua long enough! Victory over this thief, Satan, is long overdue! I say, "All Believers can defeat Satan (their true enemy) with *Manna*–the most powerful spiritual weapon in their spiritual arsenal."

Satan, "The thief comes only to steal and kill and destroy."[132] What does Satan steal? Well, John 10 says Satan steals the Lord's sheep. Satan also steals *Manna* from God's sheep. According to Jesus in Mark 4:15, Satan comes and takes away the word *(Manna)* that was sown in them."

Why does Satan steal *Manna* from the LORD's people? Because those who eat *Manna* live forever. Those who do not eat *Manna* die. Satan steals *Manna* because his life depends upon it! Eating *Manna* is a life or death matter. I wonder if Satan has a lot of "fallen angels" to feed! Satan is a fallen cherub angel. *Manna* is the food of angels. God expelled that old "father of lies," Lucifer, from heaven due to his pride. Therefore, Satan no longer has access to eat the "Word of God" and survive. God expelled him to earth where the only available source of *Manna* is that which humans are allowed to eat and store within themselves.

Satan doesn't seem to care about humans. It seems his only interest is his own survival. Apparently, he steals enough *Manna* on earth to keep himself going until he is ultimately banished. How does Satan steal *Manna?* He steals *Manna* by tempting God's people to disobey God's *Manna* thereby leaving God's *Manna* unused. Satan did this to Eve in the Garden of Eden and attempted to do it to Jesus in the Wilderness. He got both alone, and gave each the opportunity to disobey God's Word *(Manna)*. Satan basically said, "If you won't use God's *Manna,* I will." Eve gave up some *Manna,* Jesus did not! **Not obeying *Manna* eaten** was the original sin!

As one of God's people, you are at war. Therefore, "Put on the full armor of God so that you can take your stand against the devil's schemes. For our struggle is not against flesh and blood, but against the rulers, the authorities, against the powers of this dark world and against the spiritual forces of evil in the heavenly realms."[133] Your enemy is Satan and his fallen angels.

Paul told all believers, "Be strong in the Lord and in his mighty power."[134] The Lord defeated Satan's temptations by obeying God's Word *(Manna)*. All who believe can do the same. However, we are to overcome Satan's temptations–not Satan. Jesus has defeated Satan. "The reason the Son of God appeared was to destroy the devil's work."[135] Jesus has made His enemy, Satan, His "footstool."[136] He did so by defeating Satan "by His Word" that is, "the sword that came out of [His] mouth."[137]

Satan was defeated by the "sword" that came out of Jesus' mouth. The "spiritual" weapons for believers to use against Satan are listed in Ephesians 6:13-18. They are: the "**belt** of truth," the "**breastplate** of righteousness," the "**shoes** of the gospel of peace," the "**shield** of faith," and, the "**helmet** of salvation." All of these are put on to "defend" against Satan. The only "offensive" weapon listed is the "**sword** of the Spirit, which is the word of God." When Satan comes in against God's people with "fiery darts," God "floods" Satan's fiery darts by raising up the standard of the water of His Word! Water puts out fire every time! *Manna* properly obeyed defeats Satan.

Satan is currently living on the *Manna* stolen from God's people. Satan seems to leave non-believers alone. Is it perhaps that they do not possess *Manna?* Satan is a thief and *Manna*-eaters are his targets. Once one is "born-again," they become a target for Satan's temptations. When he finds them alone, he attempts to steal their *Manna* in order to keep alive. **But, there is good news!** God has promised to give His "hidden *Manna*" to everyone desirous of overcoming Satan's temptations. God doesn't want His people to just "hear" His Word–He wants them to "do" His Word. It is not "belief" in God's Word which overcomes Satan's temptations. It is when God's Word is acted upon that swords are driven through Satan–who is utterly destroyed when deprived of *Manna*.

God's Word is not "junk food." It is not intended to be eaten quickly while on the run. God's Word should be eaten slowly, line upon line, precept upon precept. The intake of God's Word should be from more than just an occasional sermon. It should be taken in and meditated upon daily. Sermons are great but they only expose minute parts of God's Word. Believers need the entire "counsel of God" that Paul preached (Acts 20:27) in order to be protected against their enemies.

Saints, there is a big difference between "fast food" and a meal slowly prepared at home. It not only tastes better, it is better for you. Home grown and home cooked vegetables bring life to the eater. So does *Manna*. The difference in the taste of home-made chicken gravy and gravy purchased at a fast-food restaurant is the difference between day and night. I know good gravy the first bite.

We call fruit, vegetables, eggs, meat and milk "food." They are all the result of: "And God said, let there be ..." That is, *Manna* is the source of everything spoken into existence in this earthly realm. *Manna* is "first generation" food. If you think raw carrots taste good, just wait until you eat the *Manna* that created them! You see, since the natural man's life is sustained by natural food, so the spiritual life of the spiritual man is sustained by spiritual food–*Manna*.

Like earthly food, we call *Manna* by other Names: Bible, Sword of the Spirit, Word of Life, God's Word, the Truth, etc. Whatever *Manna* is called, a portion is always available to any and all who request it. The correct portion of *Manna* enables all to "do" God's will and thereby overcome the temptations of Satan.

Eating *Manna* releases the "I can do all things" inside a believer. Unfortunately, the phrase "I can do all things" is usually only associated with the miraculous. It should also be associated with the mundane. For example, with God's *Manna*, "I can get my money under control," "I can be a better spouse," I can lose weight," or, "I can spend time with God." Satan tempts Saints to "waste money," "fight with their spouse," "eat the wrong foods," "not spend time with God," or, the like. It is now time to eat and then obey *Manna*. It is time to overcome Satan's temptations in the Name of Jesus! "I can do all things through *Manna* (Christ) Who strengthens me!

Apparatus

Definitions

The Old Testament is called the TaNaK by the Jews. It is "the usual collective term for the Old Testament. The term is composed of the initial letters of the [three] words *Torah* ("Pentateuch"), *Nevi'im* ("Prophets"), and *Ketuvim* ("Hagiographa" [Writings])." *Encyclopaedia Judaica, Vol. 15,* p. 790

Law	תּוֹרה	Torah	T
Prophets	נביאים	Nevi'im	N
Writings	כְּתוּבִים	Ketuvim	K

Torah

The Torah was written by Moses. It contains the five books, Genesis, Exodus, Leviticus, Numbers and Deuteronomy. The original name for each book came from the first word in each book. They were originally written on scrolls.

"In [the] beginning"   בראשית **Genesis**

"These are the names"   ואלה שמות **Exodus**

"[The LORD] called"   ויקרא **Leviticus**

"In the wilderness"   במדבר **Numbers**

"These are the words" אלה הדברים **Deuteronomy**

Nevieem

The Nevieem (plural for "nabi" Heb. Prophet) consists of 8 scrolls.

Scroll one is Joshua. Scroll two is Judges. Scroll three contains I & II Samuel. Scroll four contains I & II Kings. The scrolls are considered the "former prophets," or, the "non-writing prophets." There are stories about and quotes from certain prophets [such as Elijah] contained in these scrolls. Their names are not the "titles" on the scrolls containing their information. That is why they are classified "non-writing prophets." Since they all lived before or during King David of Israel's time, they are called "former prophets."

Scroll five is Isaiah. Scroll six is Jeremiah. Scroll seven is Ezekiel. Scroll eight contains Hosea, Joel, Amos, Obadiah, Jonah, Micah, Nahum, Habakkuk, Zephaniah, Haggai, Zechariah and Malachi. This eighth scroll is entitled "Hosea." These are the "latter prophets," or, the "writing prophets." They lived after King David and each of their books bears their own name.

Ketuveem

The Ketuveem [*Ketuvim*] consists of 11 scrolls. Ketuveem is plural and comes from the Hebrew word "katav" which means "to write."

There are three Ketuveem "poetical" scrolls. Scroll one is Psalms. Scroll two is Proverbs. Scroll three is Job.

The second classification of Ketuveem scrolls is called *Megillot.* Scroll four is the Song of Songs (Solomon). Scroll five is Ruth. Scroll six is Lamentations. Scroll seven is Ecclesiastes. Scroll eight is Esther. These scrolls are read by Jews on holidays or festivals.

The remaining three Ketuveem scrolls are the "roll" scrolls. They contain genealogical information regarding Israel. Scroll nine is Daniel. Scroll ten is Ezra/Nehemiah (considered one book). Scroll eleven is I & II Chronicles (considered one book).

The New Testament. The "New Covenant," commonly called the New Testament, is a collection of 27 books written in the first century A.D. They can be divided into three major categories–the Gospels; the Epistles; and, the Revelation. The Hebrew for "New Covenant" is ברית חדשה (B'Rith Cha-Dashah) and simply means "new covenant."

The Authors. The authors of the New Testament Books were Jews (possible exception was Luke) who were very familiar with the Hebrew Scriptures (Old Testament). Due to Alexander the Great's legacy of making Greek the official business language of the world (3rd century B.C.), these Jewish authors had their manuscripts written in Greek. It is not known if their original manuscripts were written in Hebrew. What is clear in the Greek texts of New Testament Books is the Hebrew sentence structure, idioms and terminology. At the least, the New Testament authors thought in Hebrew and translated their thoughts into Greek for the purpose of reaching the world with their message.

The Gospels are:

Matthew (written by Matthew to the Jews circa. early 60's A.D.) Matthew contains 90% of Mark–word for word.

Mark (Peter's Gospel written by John Mark to the Romans circa. late 50's A.D.) Probably written first and copied by Matthew and Luke.

Luke (written by Luke to the Greek world circa. 60 A.D.) Luke contains 75% of Mark– word for word and shares passages in common with Matthew but contains a distinct set of "parables."

Commonly called the "Synoptic" Gospels. Reveals Humanity of Christ.

John (written by John to the whole world circa. late 80's A.D.) Written by John from Ephesus.

Reveals Divinity of Christ.

The Epistles are letters written to first century A.D. churches and church leaders by the Apostles and "eye-witnesses" of Jesus Christ.

The "Living" Letter
Acts (written by Dr. Luke, who accompanied Paul)

The Letters to the Church
Romans, I & II Corinthians, Galatians, Ephesians, Philippians, Colossians, I & II Thessalonians (all written by Paul), Hebrews (author unknown - written to Diaspora Jews), James (written by - written to Diaspora Jews), Jude (written by)

The Letters to Church Leaders
I & II Timothy, Titus, Philemon (all written by Paul), I & II Peter (written by), I, II, & III John (written by)

The Book of the Revelation. "The name of the book comes from Latin *revelatio,* "an unveiling;" [and] Greek *apokalypsis,* "the removing of a veil." ... It is precisely "the Revelation of Jesus Christ" (1:1). That is, it is an unveiling of His future plan for the earth and for His redeemed saints both for time and eternity. ...

Background and Destination. The author is John the beloved (1:1). The apostle came to Ephesus around A.D. 70. He seems to have been a circuit minister at Ephesus, Pergamum, Smyrna, Thyatira, Sardis, Philadelphia, and Laodicea. He was put in prison on Patmos Isle in the Aegean in the fifteenth year of Domitian, according to Eusebius (*Ecclesiastical History* 3.18). The Apocalypse was doubtless intended especially for the seven churches of Asia (cf. 1:4 and 10-11 and chaps. 2-3). The book was also evidently intended for other churches. ...

Occasion and Date. John wrote by express command of Christ (1:10-20). ... The best date seems to be A.D. 95 or 96 (cf. Swete, Milligan, Moffatt, and Zahn). ... [John's imprisonment] was in the latter reign of Domitian, A.D. 81-96."

The New Unger's Bible Dictionary, **p. 1078**

The canonization of the Old Testament. "There is no single designation common to all Jews and employed in all periods by which the Jewish Scriptures have been known. The earliest and most different Hebrew term is Ha-Sefarim ("The Books"). Its antiquity is supported by its use in Daniel in reference to the prophets (Dan. 9:2). ... The Greek-speaking Jews adopted this usage and translated it into their vernacular as τὰ βιβλία [the Bible]. ... It is from this Hellenistic Jewish usage of τὰ βιβλία, which entered European languages through the Latin form, that the English "Bible" is derived. ...

The Canon. The term, as applied to the Bible, designates specifically the closed nature of the corpus of sacred literature accepted as authoritative because it is believed to be divinely revealed. The history of the word helps explain its usage. Of Sumerian origin, it entered into Semitic languages with the meaning of "reed" or "cane" (Heb. קנה), later used for "a measuring rod" (cf. Ezek. 40:5), both of which senses passed into Greek (κάννα, κανών). Metaphorically, it came to be used as a rule or standard of excellence and was so applied by the Alexandrian grammarians to the Old Greek classics. In the second century, κανών [kanon] had come to be used in Christian circles in the sense of "rule of faith." It was the Church Fathers of the fourth century C.E. who first applied "canon" to the sacred Scriptures. ...

The Significance of the Canon. The concept enshrined in the "canon" is distinctively and characteristically Jewish. Through it Israel became "People of the Book" and the Bible became the animating force of Jewish existence, its precepts and teachings impressed upon the mind and soul of the nation. The canonized Scriptures were looked upon as the faithful witness to the national past, the embodiment of the hopes and dreams of a glorious future, and the guarantee of their fulfillment. ... Unfortunately, there is no direct information about the origins of the canon, nor can the criteria of selectivity adopted by those who fixed it be ascertained. ... Of course, the act of canonization, in turn, served to reinforce, intensify, and perpetuate the attitude of reverence, veneration, and piety with which men approached the Scriptures."

Encyclopaedia Judaica, Vol. 4, pp. 815-826

The canonization of the New Testament. The words "New Testament" come from the Septuagint (Greek translation of the Old Testament for Jews living in Alexandria, Egypt). These Jews used the Greek word "diatheke" (διαθήκη) to refer to their collection of sacred writings considered authentic. "Diatheke" primarily means *"a valid arrangement of any sort"* but can also mean *"a covenant."* This Greek word is based upon the Hebrew word "B'rith" (בְּרִית) which is always translated *"covenant."* "It is because the Old Testament was seen as a record of God's covenant with man and the New Testament as a record of God's covenant effected through Christ that this term was appropriate in both collections. The covenant in Christ was regarded as "new" (*kaine*) as compared with the "old" (*palaia*), yet these adjectives were not intended to destroy the sense of continuity. The old was not antiquated and the new was not youthful and untried. The old was still valuable and the new was fresh in respect to man's knowledge. It was this realization of the unity between the Old Testament and the New Testament which contributed not a little to the New Testament being placed on the same footing as the Old Testament among the sacred writings of the Church. ... [The NT is called B'rith Chadashah - "New Covenant"]

One of the most characteristic features of the New Testament writers is the frequency with which they quote the Old Testament. ... This exalted view of the Old Testament canon was an important factor in the procedure of early Christian worship, since the Old Testament formed the basis for the earliest liturgies. This was true not only among the Jewish Christians, but also among the Gentiles, who accepted the Old Testament as an inspired collection. ... It will be clear that no idea of a canon of New Testament Scriptures could be conceived in the earliest period of the Christian Church, because for a time oral teaching was regarded more highly than written testimony. ... Athanasius' [A.D. 367] New Testament list [in his springtime letter to his congregation] contains the twenty-seven books of the present canon ... and described as "springs of salvation." ... The [Church] Council of Hippo [A.D. 393] in Africa agreed to a list identical with that of Athanasius. At Carthage four years after that (A.D. 397) another canonical list was agreed upon which comprised all the New Testament books."

Zondervan Pictorial Encyclopedia of the Bible, Vol. 1, pp. 731-745

Appendix

"Manna" is mentioned in the Old Testament portion of the Bible in the following locations:

Exodus 16:15
Exodus 16:31
Exodus 16:33
Exodus 16:35 (twice)
Numbers 11:6
Numbers 11:7
Numbers 11:9
Deuteronomy 8:3
Deuteronomy 8:16
Joshua 5:12 (twice)
Nehemiah 9:20
Psalm 78:24

"Manna" is mentioned in the New Testament portion of the Bible in the following locations:

John 6:31
John 6:49
John 6:58
Hebrews 9:4
Revelation 2:17

"Manna" is "every word that comes from the mouth of the Lord."
It is referred to in the Bible by the following names:

Bread of Heaven
Psalm 105:40

Bread from Heaven
Exodus 16:4
Nehemiah 9:15
John 6:31
John 6:32 (twice)

Bread of Angels
Psalm 78:25

Grain of Heaven
Psalm 78:24

Every Word
that comes from the mouth of the Lord
Deuteronomy 8:3
Matthew 4:4
Luke 4:4

In the beginning was the **Word**
and the **Word** was with God
and the **Word** was God.
The **Word** became flesh and dwelled among us.
John 1:1-14

Spiritual Food
I Corinthians 10:3

Addendum

Manna Fulfills Prophecy

Jesus was "attended" by the angels following His 40 days and nights of fasting and prayer and having been "tempted" by Satan (Matthew 4:1-11; Mark 1:12-13). "Attended" comes from the Greek word διακονως (deacon) and primarily means to "wait tables." Is it possible the angels were sharing their food (Psalm 78:25) with Him? Was this the "other food" (John 4:32) Jesus ate while speaking with the woman at the well in Sychar? After all, just like Moses and Elijah, Jesus had angels with Him to minister to all His needs (Moses - Exodus 23:20; Elijah - I Kings 19:1-9; Jesus - Matthew 4:11, Mark 1:13).

. Why did Moses and Elijah appear with Jesus on the Mount of Transfiguration? Because Jesus did not come to destroy (Matthew 5:17) the Law (Moses) or the Prophets (Elijah). He came to fulfill all they (Moses and Elijah) said. This "fulfillment" of prophecy is so exact that it is said of Moses (Exodus 33:11) and of Elijah (I Kings 19:15) that the LORD spoke directly to them–face to face as a man speaks to a man. Jesus, the Son of Man did speak face to face with these two men. The exact fulfillment is recorded in Luke 9:30. Jesus, the Lord Himself, appeared on a mountain and spoke face to face with Moses and Elijah! We even know a portion of their conversation. In Luke 9:30 it says the three discussed Jesus' "departure which he was about to bring to **fulfillment** at Jerusalem." They were talking to Jesus about how He "fulfilled" what each of their lives and deaths had prophesied!

Moses departed this earth (Deuteronomy 34:5-8) by having God Himself take him and bury him in a grave unknown until this day. Elijah departed this earth directly by God Himself as a chariot of fire taken up in a whirlwind (II Kings 2:11-12). Jesus departed this earth from the Mount of Olives in a cloud (Acts 1:9) in full view of His disciples. What a discussion! Oh, to have been present to hear that yeshiva! Peter, James and John were present and witnessed it all. II Peter 1:16-18 records Peter's reaction. He said, "We did not follow cleverly invented stories when we told you about the power and coming of our Lord Jesus Christ, but we were eyewitnesses of his majesty. For he received honor and glory [fulfilled prophecy] from God the Father when the voice came to him from the Majestic Glory, saying, *"This is my Son, whom I love; with him I am well pleased."* We ourselves [Peter, James and John] heard this voice that came down from heaven when we were with him on the sacred mountain."

The entire speech by God from heaven regarding His Son during this Mount of Transfiguration episode is recorded in Matthew 17:5. God said, "This is my Son, whom I love (Psalm 2:7 - Ketuveem); with him I am well pleased (Isaiah 42:1-2; 53:10 - Nevieem)! Listen to him (Deuteronomy 18:15 - Torah)!" God endorsed the entire Old Testament here. By selecting a portion from each section He said, "They all [the Torah, Prophets and Writings] identify Jesus as My Son, My Messiah!"

Romans 10:4 says, "Christ is the end of the law [Torah]." Most uninformed Bible students interpret this statement to mean that Jesus "ended" Moses' Law [Torah]. Never mind that Jesus Himself said in Matthew 5:17, "Do not think I have come to abolish the Law [Torah]." The Law [Torah] has not ended nor has it been replaced by the New Testament or by "grace." The Law [Torah] is fulfilled in Christ Jesus, our Lord and Savior. His own testimony regarding this is clear in Matthew 5:17.

Christ is the "end" of the Law does not mean the Law of Moses ended. Romans 10:4 begins with two Greek words τέλος γάρ (telos gar) which are translated "end" in English Bibles. "Τέλος" means "lacking nothing necessary to be complete" and γάρ is the conjuction stating "truly." Jesus truly lacked nothing necessary to complete the Law [Torah]. One could look at Jesus' life and truly see what a man looks like when he lives out Torah. Jesus is the "living" Torah. He is the "living" *Manna* sent by God from heaven to carry out God's will. And, God's Word (Jesus) returned to heaven (ascended) having "fully" accomplished God's will. Jesus did not end the Law–He perfected it! Romans 10:4 says *"Christ is the affirmed fulfiller of God's Law Who lacked nothing necessary to fulfill God's Law."* The life of Jesus consisted of doing God's will.

John 17:4 stresses that Jesus fulfilled only that which was assigned to Him by His Father. Jesus' own testimony regarding this is recorded in John 8:29. It says, "I always do what pleases him." Also, in John 14:31, Jesus said, "I do exactly what my Father has commanded me." Again, in John 12:49-50 Jesus says, "For I did not speak of my own accord, but the Father who sent me commanded me what to say and how to say it. I know that his command leads to eternal life. So whatever I say is just what the Father has told me to say." Jesus was sent from Heaven by God the Father to bring eternal life to all who would obey His words. That, in a nutshell, describes what and Who *Manna* is!

Jesus said in Matthew 5:17, "Do not think that I have come to abolish the Law [Torah] or the Prophets [Nevieem], I have not come to abolish them but to fulfill them." According to the *Theological Dictionary of the New Testament, Volume VI,* page 286, "Fulfill from the Greek πληρόω (*pleroo*) literally means 'to fill,' e.g., a bottle with water." Page 287 says, "Πληρόω is used about 70 times for forms of מָלֵא [in the Old Testament Septuagint]." It goes on to say on page 290, "מָלֵא (Hebrew mah-lah) means 'full' or better 'to make full.'" In other words, Jesus made the Law "full." The particular content of this word [*pleroo*] in the New Testament is determined 'to fulfill a norm, a measure, a promise,' 'to complete or achieve' something, and the idea of 'totality' or 'fullness' is decisive.

Finally, on page 294 it says, "The goal of the mission of Jesus is fulfillment (Mat. 5:17b); according to Mat. 5:17a this is primarily the fulfillment of the Law [Torah] and the Prophets [Nevieem], i.e., of the whole of the Old Testament as a declaration of the will of God. Jesus does not merely affirm that He will maintain the Law. As Jesus sees it, His task is to actualize the will of God made known in the Old Testament. He has come in order that God's Word may be completely fulfilled, in order that the full measure appointed by God Himself may be reached in Him. ... Jesus actualizes the divine will stated in the Old Testament from the standpoint of both promise and demand." Jesus said to His students "This is what I told you while I was still with you. Everything must be fulfilled that is written about me in the Law of Moses [Torah], the Prophets [Nevieem], and the Psalms [Ketuveem]" (Luke 24:44-45 NIV). Thank you, Bread of Heaven, for eternal life!

Footnotes

Footnotes

Chapter 1

01 Revelation 22:13 NIV
02 Colossians 1:15-19 NIV
03 II Corinthians 5:19 NIV
04 Acts 7:38 KJV
05 Matthew 18:20 NIV
06 Ephesians 1:22-23 NIV
07 Colossians 3:11 KJV
08 Ephesians 2:15b-17 NIV
09 Romans 1:16-19 NIV
10 Isaiah 49:6 NIV
11 Genesis 49:10 NIV
12 Acts 15:11 NIV
13 Romans 3:28 NIV
14 John 1:1-2 NIV
15 Colossians 1:17 NIV
16 Proverbs 8:23, 30-31, 35 NIV
17 Luke 24:27, 44b-45 NIV
18 Hebrews 9:8-9 NIV
19 John 14:26 NIV
20 I Corinthians 10:6 NIV
21 *Gesenius Heb. Lexicon*, p. 458
22 John 5:39 NIV
23 Colossians 2:23
24 *Gesenius Heb. Lexicon*, p. 710
25 Revelation 19:10 NIV
26 II Peter 1:3-4 NIV
27 Isaiah 48:17 NIV
28 Isaiah 50:4 NIV
29 Genesis 26:5 NIV

Chapter 2

30 *Encyc. Jud., Vol 11*, p. 884
31 Deuteronomy 8:2 NIV
32 *Gesenius Heb. Lexicon*, p. 449
33 *Analytical Heb. Lexicon*, p. 496

34 *Gesenius Heb. Lexicon*, p. 487
35 *Analytical Heb. Lexicon*, p. 498
36 *Op. cit.*, p. 496
37 Exodus 16:31 NIV
38 *Gesenius Heb. Lexicon*, p. 434
39 Exodus 16:8 NIV
40 Exodus 16:3 NIV
41 Revelation 21:22-23 NIV
42 Psalm 138:4-5 NIV
43 Habakkuk 2:4, 14 NIV
44 *Biblical Literacy*, p. 308
45 Ezekiel 1:25-28 NIV
46 Isaiah 40:35 - Luke 3:1-6 NIV
47 John 1:29 KJV
48 Mark 2:27-28 NIV
49 Numbers 11:8 NIV
50 Isaiah 53:10 NIV

Chapter 3

51 Joshua 1:8 NIV
52 *Defenders of the Faith*, p. 173
53 I Peter 1:10-11 NIV
54 *Zond. Pic. Enc., Vol 3*, p. 698
55 *Op. cit.*, p. 313
56 Psalm 1:3 NIV
57 Isaiah 57:19 NIV
58 Philippians 4:19
59 II Corinthians 9:10-11
60 *Zond. Pic. Enc., Vol 2*, p. 284
61 I Kings 18:21 NIV
62 I Kings 17:15-16 NIV
63 Philippians 4:19 KJV

Chapter 4

64 *Unger's Bible Dictionary*, p. 111
65 *Gesenius Heb. Lexicon*, p. 9

66 *Zond. Pic. Enc., Vol. 5*, p. 790
67 *Gesenius Heb. Lexicon*, p. 413
68 *Op. cit.*, p. 796
69 *Op. cit.*, p. 795
70 *Ill. Dic. & Concordance*, p. 226
71 *Zond. Pic. Enc., Vol. 1*, p. 790
72 Isaiah 6:6-7 NIV
73 Deuteronomy 4:24 NIV
74 II Thessalonians 1:6-7 NIV
75 *Intro. to the Old Test.*, p. 1135
76 *New Bible Dictionary*, p. 823
77 Ezra 7:10 NIV
78 Isaiah 58:13-14 NIV
79 John 14:26 NIV
80 I John 2:27 NIV
81 Nehemiah 10:29
82 II Corinthians 3:6
83 *Encyc. Jud., Vol 13*, p. 1315
84 *Ibid.*, p. 1317
85 John 1:1-2, 14 NIV
86 Isaiah 49:10 NIV

Chapter 5

87 Deuteronomy 18:15 NIV
88 Deuteronomy 18:18 NIV
89 *Gesenius Heb. Lexicon.*, p. 552
90 I Corinthians 1:22 NIV
91 Matthew 12:38 NIV
92 Jeremiah 32:21 NIV
93 Romans 16:25-26 NIV
94 John 6:29 NIV
95 John 6:51 NIV
96 Matthew 24:35 NIV
97 John 6:38 NIV
98 John 6:69 KJV
99 John 6:62 NIV

Chapter 6

100 *Zond. Pic. Ency., Vol. 1*, p. 732
101 *Ibid.*

102 *Op. cit.*, p. 966
103 *Loc. cit.*
104 I Corinthians 8:3 NIV
105 I Corinthians 8:6 NIV
106 I Corinthians 2:14 KJV
107 Colossians 2:6-7 NIV
108 *Zond. Pic. Enc., Vol. 3*, p. 87
109 *Encyc. Jud., Vol. 15*, p. 682
110 Exodus 30:10-11 NIV

Chapter 7

111 *Zond. Pic. Enc., Vol. 4*, p. 435
112 Mark 4:15 NIV
113 II Corinthians 2:11 NIV
114 II Timothy 2:24-26 NIV
115 Revelation 12:9 NIV
116 Revelation 12:12 NIV
117 Revelation 12:10-11 NIV
118 Matthew 8:16 NIV
119 Isaiah 25:8 NIV
120 *Gesenius Heb. Lexicon*, p. 788
121 Matthew 4:1 NIV
122 *Analyt. Greek Lexicon*, p. 109
123 II Corinthians 10:4-5 KJV
124 Isaiah 59:19 KJV
125 I Peter 5:8 KJV
126 I John 4:2-4 NIV
127 II Timothy 2:15 NIV
128 Ecclesiastes 12:12 NIV
129 Hosea 4:6 NIV
130 II Timothy 3:7 NIV
131 John 8:31-32, 36 NIV

Epilogue

132 John 10:10 NIV
133 Ephesians 6:11-12 NIV
134 Ephesians 6:10 NIV
135 I John 3:8 NIV
136 Psa. 110:1 & Heb. 10:13 NIV
137 Revelation 19:21 NIV

Bibliography

Analytical Concordance to the Bible, Young, Robert,
   Hendrickson Publishers, Peabody, MA 01961, 2002
Biblical Literacy, Telushkin, Rabbi Joseph,
   William Morrow and Company, Inc., New York, NY, 1997
B'Rith Chadesha (New Covenant), Bible Society in Israel,
   Lowe & Beydone Printers, Ltd., Thetford, Norfolk, UK, 1998
Compound of Hebrew, Schachter-HaHam, Mayer,
   Kiryat Sefer, Ltd., Jerusalem, Israel, 1982
Day by Day in Jewish History, Bloch, Abraham,
   KTAV Publishing House, New York, NY, 1983
Defenders of the Faith, Heilman, Samuel,
   Schoken Books, New York, NY, 1992
Dictionary of Old Testament Words, Pick, Aaron,
   Kregel Publications, Grand Rapids, MI, 1977
Encyclopaedia Judaica, Vols. 1-16, Keter Publishing House
   Jerusalem, Ltd., Jerusalem, Israel, 1978
Englishman's Greek Concordance, Wigram, George
   Zondervan Publishing House, Grand Rapids, MI, 1970
Englishman's Hebrew & Chaldee Concordance, Wigram, George,
   Broadman Press, Nashville, TN, 1980
Gesenius' Hebrew and Chaldee Lexicon, Tregelles, S. P., trans.,
   Baker Book House, Grand Rapids, MI, 1993
God in Search of Man, Heschel, Abraham Joshua,
   The Noonday Press, New York, NY, 1993
Greek-English Lexicon of the New Testament, Thayer, Joseph H.,
   Baker Book House, Grand Rapids, MI, 1977
Hebrew and English Lexicon, Brown, Driver, Briggs,
   Associated Publishers and Authors, Lafayette, IN, 1978
Hebrew Thought Compared with Greek, Boman, Thorleif,
   W. W. Norton & Company, Inc. New York, NY, 1960
I and Thou, Buber, Martin,
   Charles Scribner's Sons, New York, NY, 1958

Illust. Dictionary & Concordance of the Bible, Wigoder, G., ed.,
  Jerusalem Publishing House, printed in U.S.A., 1986
Introduction to the Old Testament, Harrison, R. K.,,
  Eerdmans Publishing Company, Grand Rapids, MI, 1987
Josephus Complete Works, Whiston, William, translator
  Kregel Publications, Grand Rapids, MI, 1978
Lexicon in Veteris Testamenti Libros, Koehler, Baumgartner, eds.,
  E. J. Brill, Leiden, Netherlands, 1958
New Bible Dictionary, 2nd Edition, Douglas, J. D., Editor-at-large,
  Tyndale House Publishers, Wheaton, IL, 1982
Strong's Exhaustive Concordance of the Bible, Strong, James,
  Thomas Nelson Publishers, Nashville, TN, 1990
Synonyms of the Old Testament, Girdlestone, R. B.,
  Hendrickson Publishers, Peabody, MA, 2000
The Analytical Greek Lexicon,
  Zondervan Publishing House, Grand Rapids, MI, 1970
The Analytical Hebrew and Chaldee Lexicon, Davidson, Benjamin,
  Hendrickson Publishers, Peabody, MA 01961, 2002
The Bible in its Literary Milieu, Maier, Tollers, eds.,
  Eerdmans Publishing Company, Grand Rapids, MI, 1979
The Bible, the Supernatural, and the Jews, Philipps, McCandlish,
  The World Publishing Company, New York, NY, 1970
The Greek New Testament, Aland, Black, Martini, Metzger,
  Wikgren, eds., Wurttemburg B.S., Stuttgart, W.G., 1968
The Holy Scriptures Hebrew and English, House, Joseph,
  S.D.H.S., Edgware, Middlesex, HA8 7LF, England, 2000
The Interlinear Hebrew-English O.T., Kohlenberger III, John R.,
  Zondervan Publishing House, Grand Rapids, MI, 1987
The Light of Life, Richman, Rabbi Chaim Simcha,
  Rachav Communications, Inc., New York, NY, 1995
The Mishnah, Danby, Herbert,
  Oxford University Press, Walton Street, Oxford, UK, 1987
The NIV/KJV Parallel Bible,
  Zondervan Bible Publishers, Grand Rapids. MI, 1987
Zondervan Pictorial Encyclopedia,Vols. 1-5, Tenney, M. C., ed.,
  Zondervan Publishing House, Grand Rapids, MI, 1977

The call of God upon Karl D. Coke to enter the ministry came at a Wednesday night prayer meeting in August, 1960 at the Coos Bay, Oregon Foursquare Gospel Church.

The call was confirmed with two important verses of scripture. The first was John17:21-"Unity of the Body of Christ." The second was Ephesians 4:12-"Equipping the Body of Christ for Ministry." Since that summer night in 1960, Dr. Coke has been focused on bringing a measurable unity to the Body of Christ and training and releasing people into ministry all over the earth. Dr. Coke has ministered on six continents, in most denominations of the Christian Church and in Jewish Synagogues. He has produced "Timothy" students all over the earth.

Dr. Coke has produced thousands of audio and video teaching tapes, written hundreds of articles for magazines, written curriculum for Bible colleges and seminaries, appeared on national radio and television programs and has taught as an adjunct-professor at Bible colleges and seminaries around the world. He has produced and conducted pastors' conferences for thousands of pastors. He has funded, produced and established the Timothy Program International campus in Muttom, Tamil Nadu, India which now trains untold numbers of church leaders in India.

For More information regarding
the Ministry of KCEA, contact:

The KCEA Staff at:
www.karlcoke.com

or

www.andybooks.com

Dr. Karl David Coke was ordained as a minister in 1964 by the International Church of the Foursquare Gospel located in Los Angeles, California. In order to offer his ministry to all denominations, he founded the Karl Coke Evangelistic Association, Inc., on July 1, 1974 in Glendale, California. The first president of this new non-profit corporation was Holland B. London, D. D., (a Nazarene minister) who was at the time Dean of the California Graduate School of Theology. The original funding for this new ministry was secured by Robert F. Dressor, Lt. Cmdr., U.S.N., Ret., who became the second president of this new ministry.

Since 1974, the Karl Coke Evangelistic Association has provided the opportunity for many independent ministries to become established in the United States, Canada, Mexico, Uruguay, India, Ghana, Brazil, England, Malawi, Botswana, Zimbabwe, Haiti and Kenya.

Dr. Coke has written and produced curriculum for Bible training on three different levels. Level one is a two-year (eight 13-week quarters) curriculum designed to educate heads of households on the basics of the Christian faith. Level one is also used to train third-world pastors who are not able to afford a "western-style" Bible college program. Level two is a four-year curriculum designed to thoroughly educate men and women in the Bible to prepare them for full-time ministry. Level two is fully accredited. Level three is a graduate curriculum designed to produce Master and Doctoral level leaders in the Church. Level three is fully accredited and stimulates the graduates to publish their theses and dissertations.

Dr. Coke is a guide in Israel and has conducted 16-day and 19-day study tours to Israel, Egypt, Jordon, Lebanon, Turkey, Greece and Italy since 1972.

For Israel Tour Information, write:
kceaoffice@aol.com

Dr. Karl David Coke was born in Rock Springs, Wyoming on November 10, 1942. He received Jesus as God's Messiah in Coos Bay, Oregon in the Summer of 1957. He married Karen Louise Johnson on December 26, 1962 in Portland, Oregon. They have two children, a son, Kary B. Coke, and, a daughter, Kristin A. Coke.

Dr. Coke graduated from L.I.F.E. Bible College in Los Angeles, California with a B. Th. in 1964 and from The California Graduate School of Theology in Glendale, California with a Ph. D. in 1974. He was the student of Dr. Butrus Abd-al-Malik who taught him Hebrew.

Dr. Coke's ministry since 1964 has been interdenominational and world-wide. He is a licensed guide in Israel and has written and established the Timothy Program International which is a 9-year, 3-tiered Bible curriculum. He has produced thousands of audio and video tapes, written articles for Christian magazines and books, appeared on national television programs, spoken at family camps and large Christian gatherings. He pastors and conducts annual pastors' conferences throughout the earth.